INNOVATIVE
CORPORATE
AND
EXECUTIVE
STRATEGY

INNOVATIVE CORPORATE AND EXECUTIVE STRATEGY

Understanding and Meeting Financial Challenges

H. GRIFFIN EWING

NELSON-HALL 🔲 CHICAGO

Library of Congress Cataloging in Publication Data

Ewing, H. Griffin   1925–
Innovative corporate and executive strategy.

Bibliography: p.
Includes index.
1. Employee ownership. 2. Corporations—Finance.
3. Estate planning. I. Title.
HD5650.E96   658.1'5   80–25687
ISBN 0-88229-545-4

CONTENTS

PREFACE

Successful multiplication of profit and personal payoff in the corporate structure comes to those who have learned, through patience and perspicacity, how to apply the arts of leadership/followership in all levels of their business relations.

Corporate financial and employee success can be likened to a data-processing center. Computers are born from the marriage of miles and miles of glass, metal, and other components that results in a complex machine—panels, switches, relays, condensers, and wires. Thoughtful perusal of the computer's manual of operational procedures would readily yield an idea of the designer's intention and of the reasons that companies install computers—the process timing, main memory time and space, and input/output analysis that provide the groundwork for quantitative answers to technical uncertainties—the groundwork for establishing short-run and long-run goals.

However, if you happened by chance or choice to look at the back side of the equipment, you would see no purpose—only the seemingly endless crisscrossing of hard material from which the machine was constructed. The back side of the computer gives no hint as to what data processing is all about. So it is with the corporate formation.

Behind the corporation's organizational chart lies another complex arrangement—a seemingly endless assortment of people, machines, property—the haves and have-nots, takers and givers, the miles and miles of paperwork intended to control and regulate, crisscrossed by channels of upward and downward communication —the physical components behind the real purpose: *corporate profitability.*

To be successful, corporations must work hand-in-hand with and support an atmosphere that encourages all levels of employees to commit themselves to doing a good job—to producing. Corporate executives must keep abreast of company projects via interaction with marketing, production, and finance if they are to evaluate and meet the challenges of competition and the uncertainties of the economy.

To those sincere searchers for a guideline to corporate profitability, who want a practical working approach to organizing pretax deductible financial plans, a better understanding of asset conservation/retention strategy—to those who want to see past the back side of the computer, to understand how management, vested interest, and employees can work together for the enrichment of all—I dedicate this book.

INTRODUCTION

AND

OVERVIEW

This book has one main objective: to help you, the searcher for financial corporate strategy, learn enough about the corporate form of cash flow leveraging so that you will be able to take advantage of opportunities you will have to build your own profit centers—as your business increases.

LEVERAGING EMPLOYEES' PRODUCTION CAPABILITIES

Increased employee awareness and commitment can help solve company problems stemming from inflation-defense economics. Therefore, the corporation can augment production, marketing, and profits by encouraging its employees to consider themselves *partners* in the enterprise and to identify more closely with the company, its management, and its special problems. Chapters 1, 2, and 3 explain this *modus operandi*.

Currently, Congress is supporting plans to make employees shareholders by giving them either stock in their own companies or cash that must be used to purchase such stock. Congressmen now realize that our nation's economy (sales, marketing, production) is strengthened only as a meaningful employer-employee relationship exists. When corporate owners share part of their company equity with those who produce the services or products, the qualities of balance and commitment become more significant. Capitol Hill has continually sought to promote profit sharing between those who contribute equity dollars and those who produce the end product. Senators Russell Long, Jacob Javits, and Mark Hatfield are strong supporters of allowing corporations to leverage tax dollars as a trade-off for stock-ownership planning, in order to afford employees a second source of income through capital ownership (see fig. 1.1). The late Sen. Hubert Humphrey also contributed to these developments.

The powerful Senate Finance Committee and the House Ways and Means Committee enthusiastically endorse the employee stock ownership trust (ESOT) concept, as demonstrated in Senator Long's March, 1976, *Fortune* magazine statement:

> Bring on those tired, labor-plagued, competition-weary companies, and ESOP (Employee Stock Ownership Plan) will breathe new life into them. They will find ESOP better than Geritol. It will revitalize what is wrong with capitalism. It will increase productivity. It will improve labor relations. It will promote economic justice. It will save the economic system. It will make our form of government and our concept of freedom prevail. . . .

On July 11, 1977, Senator Hatfield wrote the author, "As you know, I have long been a supporter of stock ownership plans for employees, and your involvement in this program is certainly to be commended. . . ." Congressman Al Ullman, chairman of the House Ways and Means Committee, wrote me the same day, "As the Ways and Means Committee considers legislation on capital formation (ESOPs) later in this Congress, I will certainly give your views my careful attention."

BACKGROUND AND REASONS FOR
GROWING POPULARITY

In 1887, the Procter and Gamble Company became the first national corporation to startle the business world by organizing a profit-sharing plan designed primarily to enable employees to invest in common stock of their company. Sears, Roebuck and Company in 1916 started its profit-sharing plan, which is still considered among the nation's finest. It, too, directed its trustees to purchase company common stock for employees, with dollars that were tax deducted.

The Revenue Act of 1921 first allowed trusts to organize and implement accounting procedures for qualified profit-sharing plans, i.e., stock-bonus plans that provided the trust complete exemption from federal taxation. The important tax-exempted status given to qualified profit-sharing plans brought with it financial techniques and strategies that increased company cash flow on the basis of dollars generated from the purchase of its own issued or unissued capital stock. Simultaneously, the plans permitted employees participation in company stock: they acquired an interest void of gift and estate taxes. Furthermore, the company was enabled to finance capital improvements by utilizing pretax dollars to pay off debt financing. The key strategy behind linking employer tax benefits with employee commitment is to permit the corporation to finance new capital growth (e.g., through IRS Section 1245–1250), while also building beneficial—and tax-free—stock ownership for employees. For example, under this arrangement, the company may add properties, retool and erect new plants, acquire or spin off a division—all with tax-deferred status.

FINANCIAL TECHNIQUES THE PLAN PROVIDES

1. The plan helps finance new-capital formation and company growth (see fig. 3.2).
2. It can be a vehicle for disposing of company stock. It creates an in-house market for stock transactions that are sheltered from public market fluctuations (see fig. 3.4).
3. The plan, properly drafted, enables the company to refinance present and future long- and short-term debt—interest *and* principal—with before-tax dollars (see fig. 1.1). ESOP's leveraging allows corporations to finance the purchase of divisions, companies, and other capital investments with pretax dollars of the *acquired* division, company, or investment (see fig. 3.3).
4. This unique method of bootstrapping the purchase price plus other equity sweeteners via negotiations with outside bankers and divesting companies is IRS approved and encouraged.
5. Under the umbrella of an ESOP, the family tax planner can more pleasantly approach such estate liquidity uncertainties as: Will there be a ready market for the stock of a deceased shareholder (see fig. 3.6)? How can we fund estate life insurance agreements by utilizing the "fresh money" created

by the plan? What is the proper way to draft buy/sell agreements in order to permit shareholders to avoid redemption reductions found under IRS Code Sections 302 and 303?

PERFORMANCE AUDIT STRATEGY

Ways of dealing with employee dissatisfaction, turnover, and lack of sincere commitment to synergism—i.e., loyal service towards a definable company profit/growth balance—are discussed in chapter 11. The risk-management interaction decision making described below illustrates how to communicate company financial projects to the nonfinancial executive effectively and profitably. The forces shaping relations between marketing, production, and return on investment to corporate shareholders are undergoing swift changes. The nonfinancial executive should learn inflation-defense techniques if he is to exercise his rights in the framework of reality, i.e., corporate profitability.

Risk management is not a new concept, but it is winning ever increasing acceptance as a necessary adjunct to a company's management decision team, e.g., chief executive officer, board chairman, and other profit-responsible executives. Corporate risk planning concerns itself with the professional treatment of conservation and retention of company assets. Today, every profit-making company must work to improve such external factors as expectations of shareholders, views of customers and community regarding the product or service, and general business climates and economic trends. Companies must also pay close attention to actual or prospective changes in regulations, laws, and public attitudes affecting their business.

Risk management by interaction decision planning is a feedback process. Information flowing through the pertinent departments— production, marketing, finance—brings to light risk uncertainties, producing intensified, rather than lessened, management awareness. As a result, the chief executive officer is enabled to examine company projects, present and future, from various perspectives and alternate positions.

CONSERVATION AND RETENTION TECHNIQUES

Merger planning techniques (discussed in chapter 13), if properly designed and implemented, instruct the reader in the practical advantages of how to value the merger from both the purchaser's and the seller's viewpoint. Gathering essential data in order to weigh the pros and cons of a merger transaction enables the financial entrepreneur to determine objectives and evaluate the feasibility of the merger transaction. The chapter examines the popular tax-free mergers and recommends, through a merger-tree analysis, how to measure the high/low totals concerning the valuation, how to structure the study, synergy pluses and minuses, trade-off amenities, and family tax planning.

Merger failures are often caused by mismatch of size and the inability of the acquired company to follow the acquirer's reasoning. Also, poor relationships due to lack of effective communication between the two companies will cause human and financial failures. Two basic classifications illustrate problems involving "boot," either in cash or other property, that require the merger strategist to adhere to various safeguards. The standards, methods, and means of protecting the interests of both the buyer and the seller are outlined.

MAXIMUM EXEMPTIONS AND ESTATE TAX CREDITS

After twenty-four months of hearings, the Federal Tax Reform Act was given birth on October 4, 1976, when President Gerald Ford signed the act into law. Most of the act's provisions became effective on January 1, 1977, making major changes in our federal estate and gift tax laws for the first time in thirty years. Chapter 14 explains how pre-estate tax designing can be profitable to the planners.

Under the new Tax Reform Act, each spouse receives a full unified credit, and for years 1981 forward, the $47,000 tax credit affords each spouse an exemption equivalent of $175,625. Equalizational estate planning, i.e., organizing and designing the two estates to balance assets between spouses, allows each spouse to leave up to $175,625 *free of estate tax* as compared to $60,000 under the old law. Estate planners should take a hard look at equalizational programming concerning this $351,250 tax-free placement. The unification procedures can increase the effective individual exemption, which will ultimately enable executors for a taxpayer who dies in 1981 to leverage tax-free transfers totalling

$525,000 with *no federal estate tax,* if the estate is left to the spouse (through maximum use of lifetime gifts to spouse, including gifts of interest in joint tenancies).

Illustration of planned versus direct distribution shows 15¼ percent more cash available to heirs through planned distribution. A complete twelve-page worksheet for family estate planning data supports chapter 14.

PART I

EMPLOYEE

STOCK

OWNERSHIP

PLANS

1

EMPLOYEE

STOCK OWNERSHIP PLANS:

PURPOSE AND

LEVERAGING STRATEGY

In our economy, business has three main purposes: (1) to afford the consumer pleasure in spending, (2) to allow the corporate shareholder to maximize a return on investment profit, and (3) to contribute to the goals of conventional economics—full employment. Various problems detract from the attainment of these goals. Three of them—employee restlessness that results in lessening productivity,[1] trends toward total unionization, and the need of having adequate retirement income benefits—can partly be solved by the corporate entity's adopting an Employee Stock Ownership Plan. The advantages of an ESOP would substantially reduce the need for public welfare because of the second income that would be generated to corporate employees by the company's annual dividend payments. An Employee Stock Ownership Plan is administered by an Employee Stock Ownership Trust (ESOT), a qualified tax-exempt financial device.

PURPOSE AND INTENT OF THE ESOP PLAN

Employee Stock Ownership Plans are not something new and untried. The first recorded company to use this unique financial vehicle was a Redwood City, California, corporation, Peninsula

---

1. Chris Argyris, *Intervention Theory and Method: A Behavioral Science View*, p. 59.

Newspapers, Inc. Today, this company, which in 1956 sold its stock, through a trust, to all eligible employees, is still employee owned and is operating very successfully.[2] More recent examples are Brooks Camera, Inc., whose founder decided to use an ESOT in selling 100 percent of his stock to his employees; E-Systems, Inc., a Dallas electronics manufacturer leveraging a plan to acquire Air Asia of Taiwan, Republic of China; Merrill Lynch, Pierce, Fenner, and Smith, which used ESOP in conjunction with a $10-million spin-off of its interest in Lionel D. Edie Co.; and Hallmark Cards, Inc., which accomplished an $8.3-million conversion of its profit-sharing plan involving over 10,000 employees. Well-known financial firms are going the ESOP route—Sutro and Co.; the First California Company, with its fifty branch brokerage firms; and Robinson-Humphrey Co. of Atlanta.[3]

The chief proponent of the Employee Stock Ownership Plan is a well-known San Francisco attorney, Louis O. Kelso. His views regarding the economic and social benefits of the plan can best be understood by reading his book concerning the economics of reality.[4] Kelso sees the ESOP as a financial tool to be used for a major restructuring of our country's economy. The heart of his philosophy, is the two-factor theory of economics, which, properly applied, could be extremely effective in increasing employee production and company profits.

BACKGROUND CONFERENCE COMMITTEE REPORTING

The Employee Retirement Income Security Act of 1975, commonly referred to as ERISA, has construed the acronym *ESOT* to mean Employee Stock Ownership Trust.[5] The term was originally limited to describing a qualified stock bonus plan that purchased a substantial block of stock in the employer company from a lender. The payment to the lender would be guaranteed by the employer corporation, which could, if required by the lender, give

---

2. Ronald M. Bushman, "Employee Stock Ownership Plans."
3. Dana L. Thomas, "Explosive ESOTs."
4. Louis O. Kelso and Patricia Hetter, eds., *Two-Factor Theory: The Economics of Reality.*
5. For more information on ESOTs, see "Exhibit 2—General Information Regarding ESOTs" in chapter 6.

security liens on all corporate properties such as real estate, accounts receivable, and Sections 1245 and 1250 properties. The obvious advantage of the one-group purchase of company stock, whether from one or more shareholders or from the company, is the leveraging benefit factor available to the qualified plan. Employee incentive and interest concerning corporate growth are also improved measurably by this type of deferred compensation plan, because the employees can rely on the company's commitment to make enough contributions to the plan each year to pay off the loan that financed the initial purchase of the large block of stock. This, in effect, enables the employees to have a funded trust and an identifiable interest in stock in the employer company, earned-out by the employees over a specific period of years. This goal is recognized in the Conference Committee Report to Section 408 of ERISA, which says in part: "Furthermore, it is understood that a frequent characteristic of some Employee Stock Ownership Plans is that they leverage their purchase of qualifying employer securities as a way to achieve transfers in the ownership of corporate stock and other capital requirements of a corporation, and that such a plan is designed to build equity ownership of shares of the employer corporation for its employees in a non-discriminatory manner."

The conferees intend that the exemption from the prohibited transaction rules, with respect to loans to Employee Stock Ownership Plans, is to apply only in the case of loans used to leverage the purchase of qualifying employer securities (and related business interests).

The Employee Stock Ownership Trust usually acquires stock either from a majority stockholder or from an estate in one block or from several stockholders in one purchase agreement (see fig. 3.7). It could also acquire stock directly from the company, when the company needs financing or immediately increased cash flow. The stock so acquired is paid for over subsequent years from contributions made to the employee trust. The corporate contributions are based on fixed percentages of participants' compensation.[6]

---

6. Marvin Goodson, ed., *The New Pension Legislation: ESOTs under ERISA—History and Analysis*, pp. 10–11.

GENERALIZATION OF AN ESOP
IN ITS SIMPLEST FORM

An Employee Stock Ownership Plan is essentially a stock bonus plan that uses borrowed funds to finance the purchase of a firm's stock for the company's employees. To establish an ESOP, in its simplest form, a company adopts a qualified stock bonus plan and establishes a qualified trust. The trust borrows money from a lending institution and invests the loan proceeds in employer stock at its current fair market value. The trust gives the lender its note, which may be secured by a pledge of the stock. For a graphic representation of the process, see fig. 1.1. The company guarantees the loan and agrees with the lender to make contributions to the trust in amounts sufficient to repay the loan. Company contributions amounting to a sum not to exceed 25 percent of the annual compensation paid to employees covered by the plan are tax deductible. If the stock held by the trust is pledged to secure the loan and the pledge agreement provides for a proportionate release of shares from the pledge as the loan is repaid, then a number of shares equivalent to each employee's commensurate share of every payment will be allocated to the employees' individual accounts. As allocated stock gradually vests, the employees become stockholders in the company.

The following example will demonstrate the operation of an ESOP. Using table A.1, General Corporate Information, is the first step necessary in qualifying the company (see Appendix A). Assume ABC, Inc., a privately held company, needs to raise $1 million to purchase new plant and equipment. ABC's management considers a conventional loan and the possibility of leasing but finds these options too expensive. ABC then adopts an ESOP, and the ESOP trust borrows $1 million. The loan, which is guaranteed by the company, is payable in level annual installments over five years at 10 percent interest. The trust uses the loan proceeds to purchase $1 million worth of newly issued ABC stock, as valued in an independent appraisal. If ABC's payroll averages $2 million and all employees are covered by the plan, the company may make annual tax deductible contributions to the trust totaling up to $300,000, which is more than enough to repay the loan. As the loan is amortized, both interest and principal payments, in effect,

FIG. 1.1. EMPLOYEE STOCK OWNERSHIP PLAN

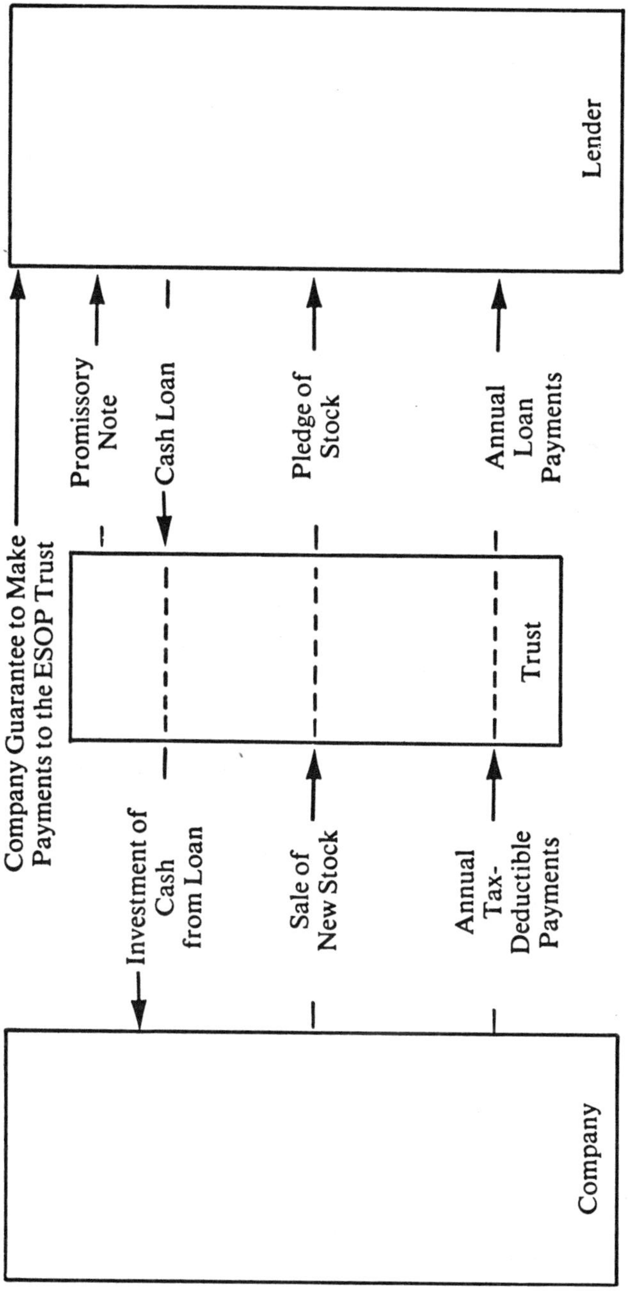

Lender

Company Guarantee to Make Payments to the ESOP Trust

Promissory Note

Cash Loan

Pledge of Stock

Annual Loan Payments

Investment of Cash from Loan

Sale of New Stock

Annual Tax-Deductible Payments

Trust

Company

When loan is amortized, cycle begins again.

will be deductible to the company, and the firm's tax liability will consequently be reduced by $720,000 over the five-year term of the loan. Meanwhile, ABC's employees will acquire a block of company stock at its appraised value at the time of sale to the trust, and all subsequent appreciation of the stock will inure to the employees' benefit. (Of course, there are also risks of depreciation.)

In addition to providing employees with stock benefits and employers with tax savings, ESOT financing reflects a new thrust in public policy. Advocates of ESOT financing view it as a means of diffusing capital ownership, increasing worker participation in corporate enterprises, and reconciling the differences between capital and labor. If the United States is ever to establish an economic counterpart to political pluralism, methods must be devised to expand ownership and increase participation in the corporate sector. The writer contends that Employee Stock Ownership Plans represent one possible means to these ends.

Because a qualified stock bonus plan forms the core of every ESOP, this dissertation will examine the statutory provisions relating to ordinary profit-sharing plans before highlighting the particular attributes of ESOPs and discussing ERISA's anticipated impact on ESOT financing. The study will then delineate the tax consequences of ESOPs to both employers and employees, and the securities regulation problems that arise in the implementation and operation of ESOPs. Consideration of a few of the possible uses of ESOT financing will follow. As evidence of the public policies underlying ESOT financing, this study will examine recent laws, aside from ERISA, that promote the use of ESOPs. Finally, the examination will show the advantages and limitations of using ESOT financing as a means of meeting future corporate capital requirements.[7]

THE IMPACT OF ERISA ON ESOPs

Although ERISA represents a massive overhaul of the entire pension system, it affects ESOPs much less substantially than it effects defined-benefit pension plans. In general, ERISA requires

---

7. Charles A. Pillsbury, ed., *Employee Stock Ownership Plans: A Step toward Democratic Capitalism*, pp. 50–53.

plan fiduciaries to administer plan investments as would a "prudent man" and to diversify the investments "so as to minimize the risk of large losses." The act exempts ESOT investments in employer stock, however, from the diversification requirement and from the prudent man rule to the extent that it requires diversification. Furthermore, ERISA exempts ESOPs from its schedule by which most employee benefit plans must divest themselves of any employer stock holdings in excess of ten percent of the fair market value of total plan assets. Finally, ERISA prevents other employee benefit plans from buying employer stock from the employer or a majority shareholder but permits an Employee Stock Ownership Trust to engage in such transactions if no commission is charged and the purchases are for no more than adequate consideration.

In addition, ERISA authorizes ESOT borrowing for the purpose of buying employer stock, although it prohibits other employee benefit plans from entering into any agreement involving the "lending of money or other extension of credit" between a plan and the employer or majority shareholder. If this prohibition applied to an ESOP, the qualified tax-exempt trust could not purchase employer stock from a majority shareholder on an installment sale basis, nor could the trust obtain a loan to purchase employer stock unless a lender were willing to make the loan without the employer's guarantee. ESOP loans and loan guarantees are exempted from this prohibition as long as the loans are primarily for the benefit of the employees and their beneficiaries, the interest rate is not unreasonable, and the only collateral used to secure the loan is employer stock.

These exceptions to ERISA's prohibited transaction rules may create the impression that the act has affirmatively encouraged ESOT financing by making advantageous changes in prior law; but, in fact, these exemptions merely preserve the law as it applied to ESOPs before ERISA. Furthermore, the fact that ESOPs are exempted from nearly all the safeguards embodied in the Employee Retirement Income Security Act of 1974 would seem to indicate congressional recognition that ESOPs, unlike defined benefit plans, are not primarily designed to provide employees with retirement income security. Indeed, this view of the statutory purpose of ESOPs is supported by a statement in the conference committee report that the purpose of ESOPs is instead "to build equity ownership of shares of the employer corporation for its employees in a nondiscriminatory manner."[8]

FINANCIAL DESIGNS REGARDING ACQUISITIONS, SPIN-OFFS, AND DIVESTITURES

The only Internal Revenue Service–approved deferred compensation plan that permits the use of pretax dollars to acquire another company is an ESOP. A cash acquisition or a spin-off may be accomplished with corporate half-dollars rather than whole dollars. A spin-off of a subsidiary company or an operating division, either due to a change of policy or because of a government-directed divestiture, can be successfully organized with ESOT financing.

The financial impact to the holding or parent company is that a built-in buyer is within the company's own financial structure. Properly organized, a divestiture or spin-off can be designed with no dilution of the parent company's earnings or equity, since the stock to be issued would be that of a new company.

Such leading management journals as the *Harvard Business Review*, and financial newspapers—the *Wall Street Journal,* and *Barron's Financial Weekly*—have shown sincere interest in the financial leveraging method being afforded the ESOT by past and present legislative enactments. The importance of the financial impact of an ESOP on a corporate debt/equity policy is the reason for the inclusion of a comparison between three forms of corporate growth.

Tables 1.1 through 1.3 and figures 1.1 through 1.3 illustrate how a $50,000 additional direct loan—obtained by the debt financing method, equity financing, or ESOT financing—relates to net income, total asset accumulation, and finally the earnings-per-share factor. The financial results shown by the three tables begin with the initial balance sheet of each financing method and extend through a ten-year calculation that graphically shows the movement of company growth through the three forms of financing. The calculation assumes that the company earns an annual 20 percent on its assets and has an effective tax rate of 50 percent.

---

8. U.S. Congress, House of Representatives, Committee on Finance, Subcommittee on ESOP Purpose, No. 98-1280, 93d Cong. 2nd Sess. 313 (1974), pp. 44–51.

The following assumptions are also used to make the test:

1. All flows and payments occur at year-end.
2. Annual earnings are retained by the company, which pays out no dividends.
3. Interest rate of 8 percent per annum at a maturity of five years refers to the ESOP loan.
4. Initially, 10,000 shares of common stock are outstanding. The ESOT buys 5,000 new shares.
5. The company applies cash flow either to current assets or to the reduction of long-term debts.
6. The market price of the stock remains constant at ten dollars per share. The mathematical reasoning is to simplify the computations of earnings per share under the treasury stock method (as relating to the ESOT financing illustration).[9]

Under these assumptions, company earnings are determined by total assets at the end of the prior year. For example, in table 1.1, Debt Financing, the company's gross income for year one is $30,000, or 20 percent of the assets shown under the starting balance sheet. Net income for year one is then $13,000 after deducting interest obligation and corporate taxes. The debt obligation, which requires a $10,000 principal payment in the first year, offsets the net income after tax, so that the actual asset increase is only $3,000 in year one. A review of the three tables is necessary in order to see how ESOT financing—using pretax income simultaneously to pay debt and to create deferred employee compensation benefits—relates to the other two conventional methods of acquiring new funds.

Table 1.3 reflects the accounting treatment of leveraged ESOPs in accordance with accounting principal Board Opinion #25. The establishment of the ESOP increases both assets and equity by $50,000. Simultaneously, however, the company incurs a fixed obligation to make a contribution sufficient to amortize the ESOT debt (shown under liabilities as "Obligation to ESOT").

The value of this benefit to both employees and employer depends upon the performance of company stock and timing of capi-

9. "ESOP's: An Analytical Report" (Chicago: Profit Sharing Council of America, 1976), pp. 29–40.

tal financing. Also, it is important to remember that corporate financing is only one aspect of an ESOP. In this writer's opinion, it is a foregone conclusion that, if capital formation is the only goal, stockholders will benefit less from an ESOP than if new shares of common stock are sold or a direct loan is made. The only exception to this rule stems from the fact that meeting SEC requirements for offering stock is sometimes costly, and as we realize, the cost of selling the stock must be considered a factor.

Tables 1.1 through 1.3 and figures 1.2 through 1.4 relate to borrowing $50,000 via three methods: debt, equity, and ESOP financing. The tables and figures are as follows:

Table 1.1 Debt Financing
Table 1.2 Equity Financing
Table 1.3 ESOT Financing
Figure 1.2 Net Income by Type of Financing
Figure 1.3 Total Assets by Type of Financing
Figure 1.4 Earnings per Share by Type of Financing

Detailed Example of Acquisition of Subsidiary by Key Management and ESOT

Assume that parent company Portland wishes to sell subsidiary Salem Company for $10 million. There is a top management team of three men, Socrates, Plato, and Diogenes, who form SPD Company; they are important to Salem Company and have been important to the parent, selling company, Portland. Salem Company has a substantial payroll and is presently operating at a profit, which Socrates, Plato, and Diogenes feel they can improve. For reasons of corporate policy, however, Portland Company wants to sell Salem Company.

The terms of sale that Portland Company works out with Socrates, Plato, and Diogenes on behalf of the new SPD Company are as follows:

Price $10 million payable $1 million down and $9 million over 10 years with interest at 5% on the unpaid balance. Payments are to be not less than 12% of the SPD Company payroll of participants in the ESOP provided, however, the SPD Company must have the cash flow to make such payments. Projections of this amount show the balance paid off in 8 years. Provisions for moratoriums are built-in, as are security devices for Portland Company. SPD Company guarantees certain mini-

TABLE 1.1. DEBT FINANCING
$50,000

STARTING BALANCE SHEET

		1 yr.	2 yrs.	3 yrs.	4 yrs.	5 yrs.	10 yrs.
Assets	$150,000	$153,000	$156,700	$161,170	$166,487	$172,736	$278,192
Liabilities	50,000	40,000	30,000	20,000	10,000	0	0
Equity	100,000	113,000	126,700	141,170	156,487	172,736	278,192
	$150,000	$153,000	$156,700	$161,170	$166,487	$172,736	$278,192

6th, 7th, 8th, 9th year not shown due to limited space.

INCOME STATEMENT

	1 yr.	2 yrs.	3 yrs.	4 yrs.	5 yrs.	10 yrs.
Gross Income	$ 30,000	$ 30,600	$ 31,340	$ 32,234	$ 33,297	$ 50,580
Other Expenses (Interest)	(4,000)	(3,200)	(2,400)	(1,600)	(800)	0
Pretax Income	26,000	27,400	28,940	30,634	32,497	50,580
Taxes	(13,000)	(13,700)	(14,470)	(15,317)	(16,248)	(25,290)
Net Income	$ 13,000	$ 13,700	$ 14,470	$ 15,317	$ 16,249	$ 25,290
No. of Shares Outstanding	10,000	10,000	10,000	10,000	10,000	10,000
Earnings per Share	$1.30	$1.37	$1.45	$1.53	$1.62	$2.53

TABLE 1.2. EQUITY FINANCING
$50,000

6th, 7th, 8th, 9th year not shown
due to limited space.

STARTING BALANCE SHEET

Assets $150,000

	1 yr.	2 yrs.	3 yrs.	4 yrs.	5 yrs.	10 yrs.
Assets	$165,000	$181,500	$199,650	$219,615	$241,576	$389,061
Liabilities	0	0	0	0	0	0
Equity	165,000	181,500	199,650	219,615	241,576	389,061

INCOME STATEMENT

	1 yr.	2 yrs.	3 yrs.	4 yrs.	5 yrs.	10 yrs.
Gross Income	$ 30,000	$ 33,000	$ 36,300	$ 39,930	$ 43,923	$ 70,738
Other Expenses	0	0	0	0	0	0
Pretax Income	30,000	33,000	36,300	39,930	43,923	70,738
Taxes	(15,000)	(16,500)	(18,150)	(19,965)	(21,962)	(35,369)
Net Income	$ 15,000	$ 16,500	$ 18,150	$ 19,965	$ 21,961	$ 35,369
No. of Shares Outstanding	15,000	15,000	15,000	15,000	15,000	15,000
Earnings per Share	$1.00	$1.10	$1.21	$1.33	$1.46	$2.36

TABLE 1.3. ESOT FINANCING
$50,000

6th, 7th, 8th, 9th year not shown due to limited space.

STARTING BALANCE SHEET		1 yr.	2 yrs.	3 yrs.	4 yrs.	5 yrs.	10 yrs.
Assets	$150,000	$158,000	$167,200	$177,720	$189,692	$203,261	$327,354
Liabilities Obligation to ESOT	50,000	40,000	30,000	20,000	10,000	0	0
Equity Total	150,000	158,000	167,200	177,720	189,692	203,261	327,354
Unearned Comp.	(50,000)	(40,000)	(30,000)	(20,000)	(10,000)	0	0
Net	$100,000	$118,000	$137,200	$157,720	$179,692	$203,261	$327,354
Total Liabilities and Equity	$150,000	$158,000	$167,200	$177,720	$189,692	$203,261	$327,354
INCOME STATEMENT							
Operating Income		$30,000	$31,600	$33,440	$35,544	$37,938	$59,520
Other Expenses (contribution)		(14,000)	(13,200)	(12,400)	(11,600)	(10,800)	0
Pretax Income		16,000	18,400	21,040	23,944	27,138	59,520
Taxes		(8,000)	(9,200)	(10,520)	(11,972)	(13,569)	(29,760)
Net Income		$ 8,000	$ 9,200	$10,520	$11,972	$13,569	$ 29,760
No. of Shares Outstanding		15,000	15,000	15,000	15,000	15,000	15,000
Earnings per Share		$ .73	$ .77	$ .81	$ .86	$ .90	$1.98

FIG. 1.2.   NET INCOME BY TYPE OF FINANCING

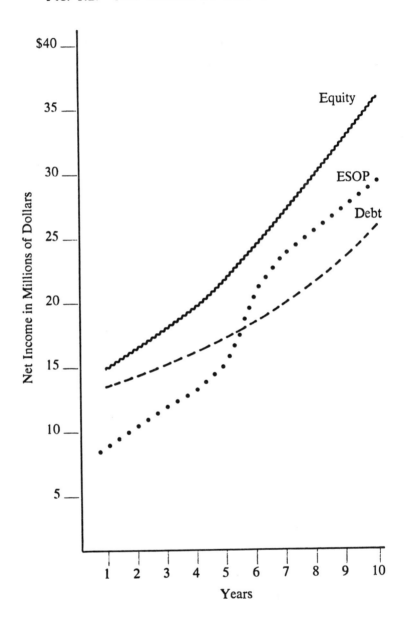

FIG. 1.3.   TOTAL ASSETS BY TYPE OF FINANCING

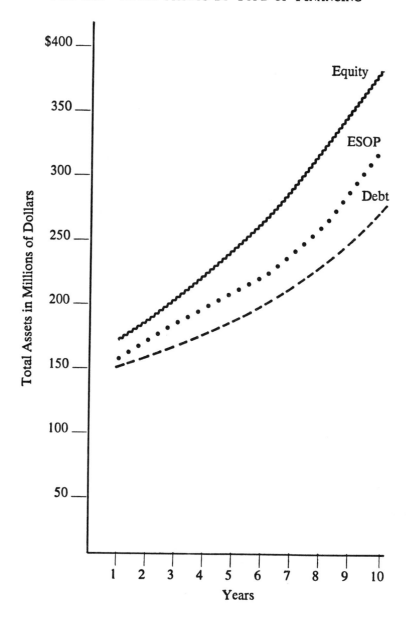

FIG. 1.4.   EARNINGS PER SHARE BY TYPE OF FINANCING

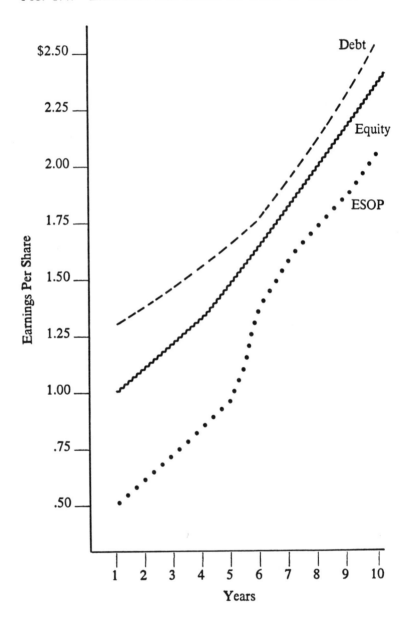

FIG. 1.5. ILLUSTRATION OF THE DEDUCTIBLE BUY-OUT
VIA 94–6 PERCENT LEVERAGING TECHNIQUE

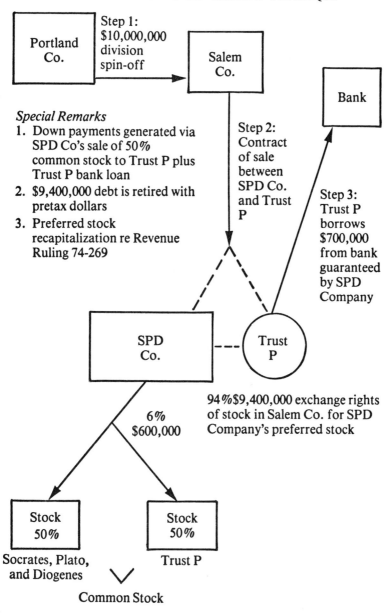

Portland Co.

Step 1:
$10,000,000
division
spin-off

Salem Co.

Bank

Special Remarks
1. Down payments generated via
   SPD Co's sale of 50%
   common stock to Trust P plus
   Trust P bank loan
2. $9,400,000 debt is retired with
   pretax dollars
3. Preferred stock
   recapitalization re Revenue
   Ruling 74-269

Step 2:
Contract
of sale
between
SPD Co.
and Trust
P

Step 3:
Trust P
borrows
$700,000
from bank
guaranteed
by SPD
Company

SPD Co.

Trust P

6%
$600,000

94%$9,400,000 exchange rights
of stock in Salem Co. for SPD
Company's preferred stock

Stock
50%

Stock
50%

Socrates, Plato,
and Diogenes

Trust P

Common Stock

mum payments. If they are not met, Portland Company can foreclose and obtain Salem Company back.

New SPD Company is formed by Socrates, Plato, and Diogenes and forms an ESOT (see fig. 1.5).

Portland Company sells its subsidiary Salem Company in one transaction to SPD Company and to the ESOT, each with an interest proportionate to the price being paid by each. The purchase price is payable $600,000 by the SPD Company and $9.4 million by the ESOT. There is separate liability. The ESOT has the right to exchange its interest in Salem Company free of lien for stock in SPD Company. One hundred percent of all SPD Company stock outstanding to Socrates, Plato, and Diogenes and to the ESOT is pledged to Salem Company with partial release clauses after the balance has been paid down to $8 million. SPD Company guarantees the ESOT payment to Portland Company.

SPD Company issues 50 percent of its common stock to Socrates, Plato, and Diogenes for $300,000 and 50 percent of its common stock to the new ESOT for $300,000. SPD Company issues $9.4 million of preferred stock to the ESOT for 94 percent of Salem Company. The ESOT borrows $700,000 from a bank, guaranteed by SPD Company. Portland Company agrees that pro rata payments can be made to the bank along with payment to Portland Company until the bank is repaid. Thereafter, all payments are applied on the note to Portland Company.

The structure of the preferred and the common must be supported by appraisals from qualified experts showing that the stock is valued properly at its issue price. This two-stock structure follows the classic pattern for a preferred stock recapitalization, which has received Internal Revenue Service approval.

Socrates, Plato, and Diogenes sign employment agreements providing they will be required to sell their common stock to the corporation in diminishing amounts each year if they do not stay employed with SPD Company. The agreement contains "substantial risks of forfeiture" as set forth in Code Section 83. Socrates, Plato, and Diogenes immediately file Section 83 elections to take into income currently any excess of fair market value over the amount paid for the stock. This ensures capital gain when they eventually sell.

Socrates, Plato, and Diogenes are now in a position to operate

SPD Company and pay the value of the acquisition in deductible dollars through the ESOT.

Simplified Structure for Acquisition of Subsidiary

The above example for SPD Company can also be set up in a simpler way as follows.

Portland Company establishes SPD Company with only common stock, exchanges 15 percent of Salem Company for 15 percent of the common stock of SPD Company, and SPD Company installs an ESOT.

The ESOT buys 85 percent of Salem Company from Portland Company for $8.5 million, payable $1 million down and the balance on the same terms as in the prior preferred stock example. The ESOT borrows $1 million from a bank, which is repayable pro rata with payments to Portland Company. SPD Company guarantees both ESOT obligations.

The ESOT exchanges its 85 percent of Salem Company for 85 percent of the common stock of SPD Company. Socrates, Plato, and Diogenes buy Portland Company's 15 percent of the common stock of SPD Company for $1.5 million on a long-term installment note. This purchase is tied in to employment contracts with substantial risks of forfeiture, and Socrates, Plato, and Diogenes make Section 83 elections.

Socrates, Plato, and Diogenes will have effective operating control of SPD Company and will have the growth leverage of a substantial asset. The ESOT will pay off its $8.5 million of obligations from contributions.

Parent Company Spin-Off Due to Narrow Margins

In 1974 Gerber Products, famous makers of baby foods, wanted to sell off a $5.5-million subsidiary called Infant Specialty Company of San Francisco. The buyers turned out to be its own employees of the Infant Specialty Company. Gerber's major reason for an ESOT financial spin-off was that this division of its operation was having too narrow margins, and a divestiture was recommended. The narrow margins hindered Gerber from utilizing this division as a spin-off investment for the public. The technique that was used for the employees to buy their own division might be referred to as a deductible buy-out (figure 1.6 explains the process

FIG. 1.6.   ESOT FINANCING
IN A CORPORATE SPIN-OFF

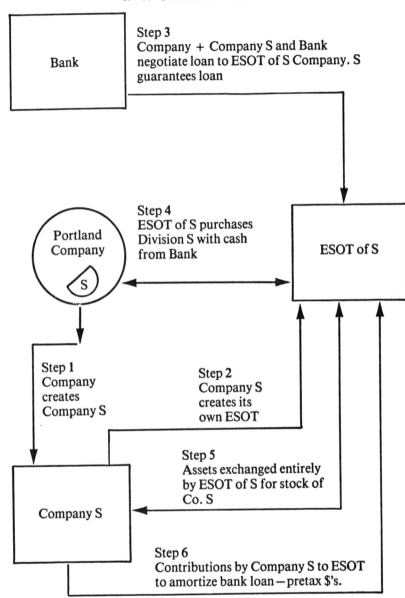

involving a company, a bank, and the financing plan). Following is an example of an ESOT spin-off transaction:

1. The division adopts an ESOT plan.
2. The ESOT borrows the money from the bank, and the loan is guaranteed by the division.
3. The ESOT (trust), by itself or together with key employees or outside investors, buys the division's stock in exchange for cash—although an installment purchase may be used. The parent company can allow the installment purchase without bank borrowing.
4. The new company (the old division) can make annual cash contributions up to 25 percent of the qualified payroll.
5. The ESOT amortizes its bank loan with the pretax cash contributions from the new company (the old division).

The advantages are as follows:

1. The parent company can receive the same price that would be paid by a third-party buyer.
2. The acquisition debt is repaid in pretax dollars, which is the main advantage of the ESOT plan for financing the divestiture of a division. This can increase the cash flow to the division, or it can make the repayment of the acquisition debt quicker or twice as secure.
3. It enables the employees in the division to acquire the division with pretax dollars and without personal borrowing.

2

CONGRESSIONAL APPROVAL

AND

ITS CONSEQUENCES

The two-factor economic theory requires the growth-oriented companies to take a look at three political-economic roads regarding conservation and retention of their assets. In December, 1973, Sen. Russell B. Long said:

> We could take the first course and further exacerbate the already intensely concentrated ownership of productive capital in the American economy, or we could join the rest of the world by taking the second path, that of nationalization, or we can take the third road, establishing policies to diffuse capital ownership broadly, so that many individuals—particularly productive workers—can participate as owners of industrial capital.[1]

Long made these remarks on the floor of the Senate, while urging his colleagues to support the provision relating to Employee Stock Ownership Plans in the legislation authorizing the reorganization of the bankrupt Midwest and Northeast railroads.

Important congressional legislation sponsored by Long, chairman of the Finance Committee, paved the way for the dollar-leveraging vehicle that, properly organized, permits an equilibrium factor concerning the United States economy. The first significant piece of legislation with this thrust was the Regional Rail Reorganization Act enacted in January, 1974.[2] It allowed Consoli-

---

1. 119th Cong. Rec. S. 22522 (daily ed., December 11, 1973).
2. 94th Cong. Rec. Vol. 121–30 (daily ed., February 26, 1975).

dated Rail Corporation, which was slated to operate the recognized Northeast railroads, authority to buy its own common stock through an Employee Stock Ownership Trust plan for all its employees. Senators on the growing list of supporters of such financing are beginning to understand the economic doctrine behind the design. Both liberals and conservatives now realize the popularity of letting workers share directly in the growth of profits, and this feature is especially appealing to the liberals. On the other hand, the concept that business, not government, should be the arbiter of its fortunes is most attractive to the American conservatives. Some proponents of this method of financing believe that it presents certain beleaguered industries with their only alternative to total nationalization. For example, Senator Long thinks that only by acquiring a stake in capital ownership will railroad workers be sufficiently motivated to put the carriers on a paying basis.

The second bill to promote such financing was the Foreign Trade Act of 1974. It provides that companies having an Employee Stock Ownership Plan will get special preferences in the $1-billion program of federally guaranteed loans to businesses located in geographical areas and/or industry groups hurt by foreign competition.

Thirdly, the new pension legislation, ERISA, singles out the ESOP as the only employee benefit plan that can be used as a vehicle for corporate borrowing and other debt-financing purposes.

The fourth bill in the series, and the one that has especially alerted business to the advantages of the plan, is the Tax Reduction Act of 1975. Besides raising from 7 percent to 10 percent the amount of tax credit a company can take for investing in Section 1245 properties, the measure provides that a firm can enjoy an additional 1 percent credit if it contributes the extra tax savings to an ESOP.

The Capital Cost Recovery Bill that is presently being argued by the Senate Finance Committee would continue the investment tax credit indefinitely at a 10-percent rate; however, it would provide credit at 12 percent when an amount equal to an additional 2 percent was contributed to an Employee Stock Ownership Plan. The investment tax credit applicable to energy use property is also being programmed to permit the 12 percent investment tax credit for waste-burning and recycling equipment, oil shale conversion equipment, coal slurry pipelines, coal liquefaction and coal gasification equipment, etc. An investment tax credit would be also forthcoming if an equivalent amount of stock were put into an Employee Stock Ownership Plan.

Currently, the senators and representatives who support the intent and purpose of the ESOP under the accelerated Capital Formation Act of 1975 desire that even greater benefits for the employee trust users be permitted. For example, the House Ways and Means Committee is introducing bills such as the one structured by Rep. Bill Frenzel of Minnesota, which would abolish the ceiling on tax-deductible payments into an ESOT. It proposes that the company be allowed a tax deduction for contributions limited only by its capacity to service debts out of cash flow. Presently, there is hardly a government representative on Capitol Hill who is not well versed on the purpose and intent of the Employee Stock Ownership Trust. In fact, this writer believes that in the very near future the acronym ESOP will be a plank in either the Democratic or Republican platform.

PENDING CONGRESSIONAL LEGISLATION

Bob Packwood, United States senator who serves on the powerful Finance Committee, communicated with the writer on July 19, 1976, requesting his views and opinions concerning present tax legislation. Packwood wrote:

> As you know, the Congress has been considering some substantial revisions to the Tax Code. As a member of the Senate Finance Committee, I'd like to know your views on this important and controversial legislation.
>
> Congress is now returning from a two-week recess. Senator Long, Chairman of the Committee, is conducting three additional days of hearing on the Senate version of the tax revisions. His action is a response to verbal attack on the Committee Bill by a few adamant "tax reformers" including Senators Kennedy and Proxmire. In short, battles in our Committee and on the Senate floor are inevitable. Finally, the Conference Committee will be charged with the difficult task of resolving the differences between the House and Senate version of tax reform.
>
> Enclosed is a brief comparison of the Bill as passed by the House of Representatives and the Finance Committee. Your expertise and opinions on these provisions will help me deter-

mine the merits of different proposals. I hope you can spend the time necessary to fully explain your position.[3]

Packwood described the House of Representatives and the Finance Committee proposals, two major pieces of tax legislation that have an important bearing on ESOPs.

Capital Cost Recovery—Energy
September 30, 1978

Revenue Act of 1978

(a) *Investment Tax Credit*—Extends through December 31, 1983, the 11% investment tax credit and the $100,000 limitation on qualified investment in used property.

(b) *Investment Tax Credit for Energy Use Property*

Senate Finance Committee Version

(a) *Investment Tax Credit*—Continues investment tax credit indefinitely at 11% rate; provides credit at 11½% where amount equal to additional ½% is contributed to an Employee Stock Ownership Plan (ESOP); permits additional carry forward for credits which otherwise have expired in prior tax years; provides numerous modifications relating to ESOPs.

(b) *Investment Tax Credit for Energy Use Property*—Provides for a 10% investment tax credit in lieu of the regular investment credit for the following: waste burning and recycling equipment (5-year period); oil shale conversion equipment; coal slurry pipelines and coal liquefaction and coal gasification equipment (10-year period); deep-mining coal equipment (5-year period); equipment used to convert organic material into methanol or other fuel that can be substituted for conventional fuels (5-year period); and equipment installed in business, commercial, and residential structures which permits the use of geothermal heat energy. In each case, there would be an additional 1% credit if the equivalent amount of stock were put into an Employee Stock Ownership Plan.[4]

---

3. Sen. Robert Packwood to author, July, 1976.
4. Robert Packwood, "Minimum Tax, Limitations on Artificial Accounting Losses and Related Provisions," review and research letter, July, 1976.

COMPETENT AND EFFECTIVE ORGANIZATIONS
SUPPORTING THE PLAN

Recently, Hallmark Cards, Inc., set up an Employee Stock Ownership Plan to spread ownership of the firm among its ten thousand workers. For years the big maker of greeting cards had operated a profit-sharing plan, which took a large reduction in value during the 1973-74 bear market. By contrast, those were among the most financially rewarding years for Hallmark; as a result, the value of its own stock, which is not publicly traded and so was insulated from Wall Street, rose approximately 10 percent in years 1973 and 1974. In an effort to improve performance of the profit-sharing plan, Hallmark converted it into an ESOP by contributing in excess of 400,000 shares of its own stock from 1974 profits. The shares contributed were valued at more than $8.3 million, which amounted to 21 percent of the trust holdings. The balance that has been maintained in the trust portfolio is in a diversified list of equities. Hallmark's use of an Employee Stock Ownership Plan in essence enabled the company to:

1. obtain cash for working capital or other purposes of approximately $4 million plus;
2. save federal corporate taxes in excess of $4 million;
3. increase its net worth for balance sheet purposes by leveraging its own inside tax dollars.

The Hallmark family, who are the principal owners of the stock of the company, have prepared legal buy/sell agreements between themselves and the trust so that their estates will eventually be able to sell the trust more than 65 percent of their shares, which will at that time give the Employee Stock Ownership Trust a 30 percent interest in Hallmark. The current president, Donald J. Hall, has stated that the absence of a public market for Hallmark shares does not present a problem for its workers; they are able to sell their holdings back to the Employee Stock Ownership Trust at a previously agreed-upon formula. The acting trustee of the Hallmark stock plan is the United States Trust Company of New York. The asset values in the trust were over $40 million at the 1974 year-end accounting. Presently, Hallmark's goal is to convert more of such assets into company stock. The tax benefits in estate planning relating to Internal Revenue Code Section 302—redemptions not taxable as dividends—and 303—distributions in redemption of stock to pay death taxes—are obviously related to the intent of Hallmark's present and future dealings with the profit-sharing trust.

The Hallmark management team also has considered the important strategic response to ERISA concerning the numerous options available to the company through an ESOP and not available through other qualified plans.

A staff reporter of the *Wall Street Journal* on February 24, 1976, stated that—

> Merrill Lynch & Co. agreed in principle to sell certain parts of its Lionel D. Edie & Co. investment advisory unit to the Edie employees.

As of the writing of that date, Merrill Lynch declined to disclose the terms of the prospective transaction, but the sale price was estimated at $10 million. Merrill Lynch, the large financial services holding company, said,

> The divestiture is being prompted by recent Federal Legislation calling for the separation by mid-1978 of certain money-management and security brokerage activity.

The agreement tentatively called for the sale of Edie's pension fund investment counseling activities; management rights to the Edie Special Growth Fund, Inc., mutual fund; and the Lionel D. Edie & Company name. The parts to be sold would be purchased by a stock ownership plan (ESOP) that was to be formed on behalf of the Edie employees.

On June 2, 1976, the same staff reporter published another newsworthy item disclosing more facts regarding this financial divestiture. He mentioned that Merrill Lynch & Company put an $8.4 million price tag on the portion of the Edie & Company subsidiary that it was selling to Edie employees under an ESOP. Under the plan, Edie's Employee Stock Ownership Trust would purchase, over a ten-year period, Edie's investment-counseling activities for pension funds; the management rights to Edie's Special Growth Fund, Inc., mutual fund; and, as previously mentioned, the Edie name. It is interesting to note that a 12-percent interest rate would be paid on the unpaid balance of this $8.4-million agreement.

The author contacted Merrill Lynch and Company and was informed that the contract obligation could be prepaid at any time, so that interest payments could not be estimated. However, assuming the $8.4 million is paid in equal installments over a ten-year debt retirement plan, the interest factor would approximately equal the purchase price. The Merrill Lynch representative also stated that, even though the Internal Revenue Service letter of approval qualifying the ESOP had not yet been received, the Edie Company would be spun off by July 1, 1976, and operate as a separate entity. By applying a discounted cash flow method to determine the value of the dollars being put to profitability by Merrill Lynch, including a delayed factor of not using these inside dollars, one finds an enormous leveraging factor that is being used by the big companies such as Merrill Lynch and Hallmark Cards. The discounted cash flow method rests on the time-honored maxim that money begets money. The fact that dollars on hand today invested in profitable projects yield additional earnings to an investing company is, to this writer, the major reason for the divestiture by Merrill Lynch & Company. Comparing this move with a delayed-action move of waiting until some future date to invest a dollar, all alert businessmen thoroughly understand that no earning power would be derived in the interim. Consequently, the forward-minded companies today have placed a time value on their money. A dollar in the bank today is much more valuable than one to be received at some future date.

South Bend Lathe was a recent unique spin-off from Amsted Industries that affected approximately $10 million and five hundred workers. The assistant secretary of commerce for economic development authorized a $5-million government loan for the city of South Bend, matched by another $5.1 million from private lenders, thereby enabling the employees to buy the subsidiary from the mother company. The government loan had a twenty-five–year amortization scheduling at a modest 3 percent rate of interest and has been termed a unique and novel financial vehicle. This transaction was allowed under the internal revenue code relating to qualified employee stock ownership trust plans. The unique part of this spin-off was the 100-percent-deductible buy-out method of approach, the first of its kind involving the public use of this type of financing, in order to lessen the high-unemployment problems that have been cropping up as a result of the link between productivity and corporate growth. Properly designed, the Employee Stock Ownership Trust is a vehicle that can use pretax dollars, not only to raise new cash, but also for refinancing existing debt. The most popular use of the pretax-dollar approach to conservation and retention of corporate assets is to use these dollars to finance acquisitions and corporate divestitures and to spin off a division or a subsidiary.

E-Systems, Inc., on January 31, 1975, acquired Air Asia Co., Ltd., as a wholly owned subsidiary. Prior to the acquisition, Air Asia, which had its principal place of business in Taiwan, Republic of China, was being operated as part of Aircraft Systems Group of E-Systems, although it did not constitute a material part of the business or assets of E-Systems. Air Asia is a competent, highly respected aircraft modification, maintenance, manufacture, and servicing firm. It has modern, completely equipped facilities to perform such business and has an excellent reputation for high-quality, cost-effective service work in the Far East. Air Asia employs in excess of twenty-eight hundred employees, many of whom are highly skilled airframe and engine mechanics, electronics technicians, or engineers.

E-Systems, Inc., adopted, designed, and approved an Employee Stock Ownership Plan, and its shareholders at its annual meeting of April 4, 1974 supported this financial vehicle. The purpose, besides dollar leveraging, was to increase employee productivity and reduce turnover. The design is basically aimed at furnishing employees additional benefits upon retirement in the form of a distribution of E-Systems common stock accumulated throughout their career with the company. Every employee of E-Systems (excluding employees of its subsidiaries) is a participant in the plan, which is entirely paid for by the company. It is interesting to note that, immediately following the shareholders' approval of the plan during April of 1974 the trust completed a public tender offer for approximately 500,000 shares of the company's common stock. The notes to financial statements of E-Systems, Inc., pointed out that funds were borrowed to complete the public tender offer and that the company effectively was obligating itself to contribute to the employee trust in an amount sufficient to repay the loan in installments over a seven-year period. The obligation for future contributions would be reflected in the balance sheet, with an equal amount shown as a deferred employee benefit. Of course, the contributions to the trust are tax deductible and are accounted for by the company in the same manner as all other employee fringe benefit expenses, which are included as overhead costs in establishing prices and not funded directly out of profits. The notes to the financial statement concluded by saying that contributions to the trust would not cause a future adverse effect on the company's income. Contributions to the trust for the year ending December 31, 1974, were $1,278,000.

Smaller companies also benefit. A West Coast manufacturer, Ultra-Violet Products of San Gabriel, California, also has such a plan. Paul Warren, president of the $3-million-a-year manufacturing concern, described how it was working:

> It has helped the employees, helped the original stockholders and it has helped management.

Warren's father started the ESOP in 1973 in order to finance a 60,000-square-foot expansion. By 1978, when the original loan would be paid off, Ultra-Violet's eighty employees were expected to own one-third of the company.

Warren, who with his father owned a controlling interest, continued his testimony:

> It has made our people much more aware of the company and its problems. . . . I can't say they're actually working harder, but as part owners, the employees really seem to be taking an interest.[5]

Warren went on to mention that Ultra-Violet had saved thousands of dollars because of the special tax shelter involved with ESOPs. The writer has had a similar experience with a small company that has just finalized its plan.[6] It's a 90–10 deductible buyout in which three of the executives of the firm bought 10 percent of the outside stock of a subsidiary to the mother company, which enabled them to have management control. The 90-percent balance was simultaneously bought by an ESOP trust, which enabled the SBA to work with a local bank to finance the 90 percent stock purchase by the employee stock trust. This plan con-

5. Quoted by John Getzee in the *Los Angeles Times*, April 6, 1975.
6. See Appendix B for a representative list of companies that have adopted ESOPs.

sisted of a twenty-five–percent maximum contribution allowance, commonly referred to as an ESOP money purchase plan. The twenty-five–percent leveraging factor that is permitted under a combination trust plan was necessary in order to retire the large loan within a ten-year period of debt scheduling. Under the conventional method of borrowing money to purchase the firm, banks and financiers would not have been able to finance the purchase, since there was not sufficient cash flow being generated with after-tax dollars. Utilizing inside dollars, such as the deduction being afforded for contributions paid into the trust, enabled the 90–10 deductible buy-out plan to be designed, organized, and implemented. Expending pre-tax dollars instead of retained earnings obviously provides a two-to-one ratio of leveraging power. To avoid the 50 percent corporate tax by using these inside dollars to acquire a subsidiary or in a divestiture or spin-off plan is a business activity that never before has had a cover position—but it is now permitted under the 1975 Tax Reduction Act.

Hewitt Associates recently prepared for the Profit Sharing Council of America a study that involved reviewing in depth ten companies that had established ESOPs over the previous four years. The companies in the study ranged from $3 million to $1.5 billion in annual gross sales, and total covered employees in a company ranged from fewer than 200 to over 10,000. Of the ten companies, only five had utilized the ESOP design as a corporate finance technique. Four out of these five said that a major objective of their plan was to increase employee incentive, which in turn was an instrument to lessen the turnover problem as well as to encourage increased productivity and support to the corporate entity. One major firm mentioned the plan's availability as an estate-planning mechanism. Employee enthusiasm and response to the intent and purpose of the plan were the major reasons that four of the companies put a plan into operation. The five companies that did not consider the trust as a financing vehicle also listed employee incentive as a major reason for designing the plan.

The Hewitt Associates survey was merely responding to the limited number of ESOPs considered in relation to various achievements. It is commonly thought that the major reasons that corporate officers or directors adopt a stock-bonus plan are (1) to provide a market for the closely held company stock; (2) to make capital financing tax deductible; and (3) to provide for cash-free deductions. The survey, however, pointed out the importance of a qualified plan as a superior employee-incentive device. Employee Stock Ownership Plans give employees a direct, invested interest in the success of their company, enable them to share in the profits of their own labor, and create an identity of interest between management and labor.

3

FINANCIAL INCENTIVES

FOR THE COMPANY

TO ESTABLISH A

TAX-DEDUCTIBLE PLAN

A major reason for a corporation to establish an Employee Stock Ownership Plan, or any other qualified employee benefit plan, is the tax incentive. Briefly, tax deductions are provided for employer contribution to an ESOP, and, under the Tax Reform Act, a tax credit is available for companies establishing the investment-credit ESOPs.

To establish optimum procedures and methods, one must take a strong look at present benefits afforded a plan under a profit-sharing structure as compared to the tax-leveraging advantages permitted by ERISA laws and regulations. The single most-typical reason for a company to establish an ESOP rather than a profit-sharing plan is to benefit the owner's estate-planning position—i.e., through the sale of his business to a third party to derive cash flow and long-term capital gains benefits. The key distinction between inside corporate dollar leveraging as compared to spending aftertax retained dollars can best be understood through comparative analysis of various plans permitted under current legislation. (For some graphic comparisons, see fig. 3.1.)

JKL, Inc., has adopted a qualified profit-sharing plan for its eligible employees. It has a participating payroll of $750,000, and JKL, Inc., annually contributes the maximum 15 percent of payroll to the plan. JKL, Inc., is in the 50-percent tax bracket.

FIG. 3.1. CASE NO. 1: QUALIFIED PROFIT-SHARING PLAN
VERSUS ESOP PROFIT-SHARING DESIGN

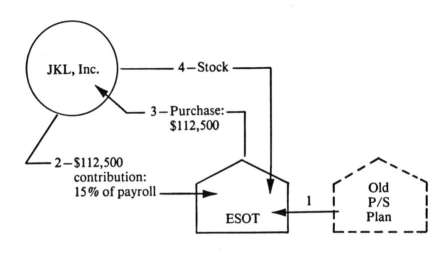

Costs and Benefits of Profit-Sharing Plan versus No Plan

	Annual Contribution	Aftertax Cost	Effect on JKL Net Worth
With Plan—$112,500	$56,250	($56,250)	
Without Plan—$0	$0	$0	

Costs and Benefits of Profit-Sharing Plan versus ESOP Plan

	Annual Contribution	Aftertax Cost	Effect on JKL Net Worth
Profit Sharing	$112,500	$56,250	($56,250)
ESOP	$112,500	$56,250	$56,250

KEY DISTINCTIONS BETWEEN ESOP AND A PROFIT-SHARING PROGRAM

The major differences between profit-sharing plans now existing and the qualified Employee Stock Ownership Plan are as follows:

I. Eligibility, participation, and vesting. No design differences. All the rules that apply to the profit-sharing plans are applicable to the Employee Stock Ownership Plan.

II. Contributions. The same rules regarding limitations on annual addition and deductibility that apply to profit-sharing plans are applicable to ESOPs. However, where the ESOP is engaged in financing a transition, a provision should be added that requires employer to contribute no less than the amount required to make the annual installment payments on the loan. As with profit-sharing plans, employer contributions can be made in cash, company stock, or other property. However, the ESOP should provide that, to the extent the trust needs cash to make annual installment payments on a loan, the contribution must be in cash.

III. Investment of trust assets. Generally, ESOPs provide that employer contributions will be used as follows:
  A. To make annual installment payments on the loan
  B. To purchase additional shares of company stock
  C. To purchase "key-man" employee life insurance
  D. To make other outside investments

There are also important differences between a qualified profit-sharing plan and an Employee Stock Ownership Plan relating to financial benefits resulting from special breaks in federal legislation, and these are of timely importance.

ESOT Can Borrow

The Internal Revenue Service allows a qualified trust to borrow funds to purchase investments in the employer unless this privilege is abused—for example, by the trust's borrowing funds to invest in an employer that is bankrupt. The revenue ruling states:

> There is no prohibition in the Code or in the Regulations promulgated here and under against a trust borrowing funds to purchase investments. The borrowing of funds by a trust and

investing them in the securities of, or entering into transactions
with, the employer or an entity closely related to the employer,
does not disqualify trust as one of the exclusive benefits of employees unless the borrowing is undertaken for the purpose of
benefiting the employer as, for example, borrowing in order to
furnish capital or property for use in the employer's business at
a time when the employer's financial condition is such that it is
unable to borrow money from usual financial sources.[1]

Proponents of ESOT financing have strongly emphasized the
dollar-leveraging factor that allows the ESOT, in effect, to use
pretax dollars to repay its borrowings (i.e., the employer corporation receives the tax deduction for contributions to the trust, which
funds are used by the ESOT to repay its borrowings). The obvious
conclusion is that, because of this ability to borrow, additional
methods of utilizing the ESOT are available. The legislation affords the attractiveness of leveraging pretax deductions to retire
a loan, and this has required companies that presently have a
profit-sharing plan to take a strong look at converting their plan
to an employee stock ownership design. (For illustration of the
advantages of leveraging with an ESOP, see fig. 3.2, table 3.1, and
fig. 3.3. The right to borrow is given to the ESOP, and it has recently been taken away from other profit-sharing plans and pen-
sions that have heretofore been able to borrow from their source
—i.e., to invest and use the dollars for estate planning as well as
corporate expansion. The present Employee Retirement Security
Act imposes excise taxes on those parties-in-interest who participate in prohibited transactions. What this means, in essence, is that
only an ESOP is now able to use the borrowing privileges that
heretofore were allowed pension and profit-sharing plans and that
enable companies to invest in their own stock. The leveraging
factor of borrowing has been taken completely out of the qualified
plans except those plans that qualify as an ESOP.

ESOT Invests Primarily in Employer Securities

Dollars invested in an ESOT may be invested in normal securities by banks or insurance companies as in a conventional profit-
sharing plan, or they may be used to buy shares of stock from

---

1. Rev. Rul. 71–311, 1971–2 CB 184–185.

stockholders or from the corporation itself (see fig. 3.4). Restrictions against the latter kind of dealing found in Section 503(g) of the Internal Revenue Code do not apply as stringently to ESOTs because the purpose of a stock-bonus trust is to invest in shares of the employer corporation. Since the acquisition of employer stock is the intent and motivating purpose of an ESOP, ERISA largely exempts the plan from the diversification-of-investment requirements. The only major requirement for plan investments stipulated by ERISA that is applicable to a qualified plan is that the cost of investment in employer stock must not exceed its fair market value.

ESOT Creates an In-House Market for Company Stock

Quite often we are finding today that controlling shareholders desire to sell a part of their shares in their corporation in order to diversify their holdings or to provide liquidity for investments or estate-planning purposes. Usually, however, there is no market for the sale of a minority interest in a closely held company. The ESOT solves the problems pertaining to an in-house market by serving as a readily available purchaser of shares from controlling shareholders.

A great deal of flexibility is permitted in structuring sales to the ESOT. (For examples, see figs. 3.5, 3.6, and 3.7.) If a major shareholder desires immediate liquidity, the trust may obtain a bank loan and purchase the shares for cash. If the shareholder does not need ready cash, he may minimize capital gains tax by selling his shares to the trust on an installment basis or by selling only a portion of his shares to the trust each year. The difference between a serial sale and an installment sale is generally that under a serial sale, the portion of stock sold each year is valued at the current fair market value at the end of the accounting year. If the serial sale is used instead of the installment method, it will probably take several more years for the company to buy all the stock, since the value of the remaining shares will in all likelihood increase yearly.

The creating of an in-house market through an ESOP is explained in the following example. Shareholder Brown, who owns 100 percent of the stock of Company X, which has a fair market value of $1 million, desires to sell part of his stock in order to create liquidity for estate tax purposes. Brown wants $490,000 for 49 percent of his stock in the corporation. No outside purchaser has shown interest in being a minority owner of the corporation, for reasons that are self-explanatory. If Brown causes his Company X to redeem a minority part of his stock, i.e., the 49 percent that he desires to sell, the redemption proceeds would be taxed as ordinary income dividends under Section 302(d) and Section 301 of the Internal Revenue Code. Also, it is important to note that the redemption price paid by Company X would have to be generated from its retained earnings in aftertax dollars. On the other hand, Company X could acquire the stock from the major shareholder with pretax dollars by establishing an Employee Stock Ownership Plan. The tax-exempt trust formed by the ESOP would borrow the $490,000 from a bank; however, to assure the bank of payment, Company X would guarantee the total loan to be paid as per loan agreement. The Employee Stock Ownership Trust would then purchase the stock from shareholder Brown for $490,000 cash, resulting in a capital gain tax situation for Brown. Thereafter, Company X makes tax-deductible cash contributions to the employee trust so that it can repay its loan from the bank. The obvious benefits of paying through the trust instead of the corporation is that pretax dollars are used; therefore, the principal amount of the loan is being paid with inside corporate dollars and not aftertax retained earnings cash flow.

One of the common problems of a shareholder in a closely held corporation is the present or future need to dispose of part or all of his stock in order to achieve estate liquidity or diversity of investment. Frequently, there is no market for the closely held stock short of selling the entire business. In the case of a total ownership position such as a family corporation, a stock redemption may not be an acceptable alternative because the entire proceeds of such redemptions may be treated as dividends under Section 302(d) and 301, particularly taking into account Section 318—Attribution Rules. Even if an arrangement to avoid dividend treatment can be worked out, the redemption does of course involve the purchase of the shareholder's stock with aftertax dollars of the corporation.

One motivating force that is currently leading major shareholders to consider selling closely held stock to an ESOP is that, properly planned, arrangements can be made whereby control is maintained until the total amount owed for the stock is paid (see fig. 3.8). The use of an irrevocable proxy maintained by the seller until the total installments have been paid in full, properly designed, can permit major stockholders to cash out, receive capital gains benefits, and yet retain all their original voting powers until the purchase price has been paid in full. Regarding the sale of stock by the estate of the shareholder, it is important to note that a sale can be made either independently or in conjunction with a Section 303 redemption of stock by the corporation.

FIG. 3.2.   CASE NO. 2: DEBT/EQUITY LIMITATIONS
AS APPLIED TO CASH FLOW AND
AMORTIZATION ANALYSIS

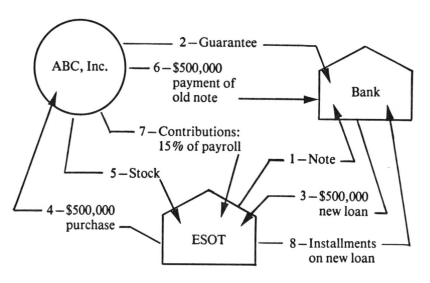

In the above illustration, ABC, Inc., already owes $500,000 to the bank. Monthly payments at 6 percent interest are to be paid over a five-year term. ABC, Inc., has income taxed in the 50 percent bracket, state and federal.

Maximum leverage permits both principal and interest payments by ABC, Inc., as a pretax dollar payout. Conventional borrowing necessitates aftertax dollars, which would require twice the cash flow.

TABLE 3.1. MONTHLY PAYMENTS AND PRETAX EARNINGS NEEDED IN CASE NO. 1, WITH AND WITHOUT AN ESOT

CONVENTIONAL BANK LOAN

Payment No.	Principal	Monthly Payments Interest	Total	Pretax Monthly Earnings Needed
1	$7,167	$2,500	$9,667	$16,834
**				
60	$9,618	$ 49	$9,667	$19,285

RENEGOTIATING THE BANK LOAN WITH AN ESOT

Payment No.	Pretax Monthly Earnings Needed Without ESOT	With ESOT
1	$16,834	$9,667
**		
60	$19,285	$9,667

NOTE: The debt/capitalization-ratio test regarding flexibility, risk, and control is minimized by pretax deduction of the principal payment.

FIG. 3.3. CASE NO. 3: ACQUIRING A SUBSIDIARY

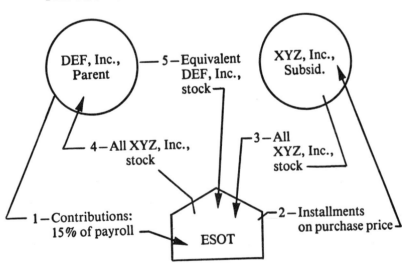

DEF, Inc., is acquiring all the stock of another corporation for cash. DEF, Inc., is in the 50 percent tax bracket. The trust accomplishes the acquisition with half-dollars instead of whole dollars.

Price of Acquisition	Pretax Earnings Needed to Acquire	
	Without ESOT	With ESOT
$500,000	$1,000,000	$500,000

Fig. 3.4.   Case no. 4: Reversing Public Offerings

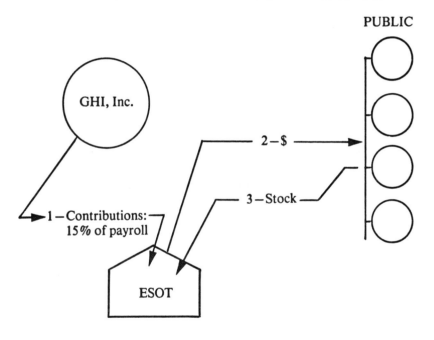

GHI, Inc., "went public" a few years back, with 40 percent of its stock registered and being traded sporadically over the counter. The founding stockholders are now disenchanted with the marketplace and plagued by the accounting and reporting requirements of the SEC and state regulatory agencies. As a result, GHI, Inc., has embarked on the reacquisition of its public shares. It is in a 50 percent tax bracket.

Shares to Acquire	Average Price per Share	Pretax Earnings Needed to Acquire	
		Without ESOT	With ESOT
40,000	$8	$640,000	$320,000

FIG. 3.5. CASE NO. 5: SALE OF BLOCK OF CLOSELY
HELD STOCK TO PERMIT DIVERSIFICATION

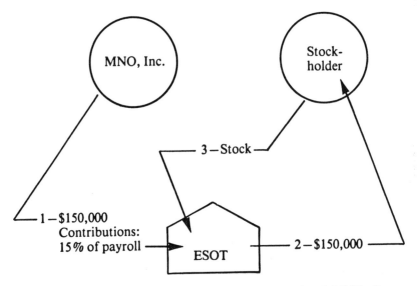

Stockholder A owns 100 percent of the stock of MNO, Inc.,
and his personal balance sheet looks like this:

Cash	$ 10,000
General Securities	6,000
Investment Realty	12,000
MNO Inc.	1,000,000
Home	75,000
Other	15,000
	$1,118,000

Case No. 5 illustrates how stockholder A could remove
$150,000 surplus liquid funds from MNO, Inc. This 15 percent
reduction would be taxed at capital gains rate, permit diversification, and free corporate surplus cash.

FIG. 3.6.   CASE NO. 6: ASSURING ESTATE LIQUIDITY
THROUGH AN ESOT RATHER THAN A
SECTION 303 STOCK REDEMPTION

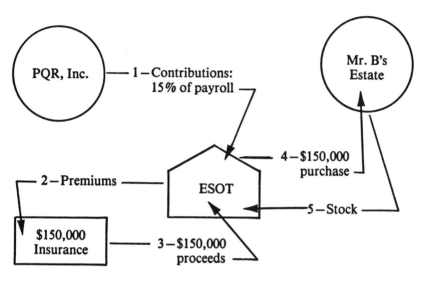

Mr. B owns 60 percent of PQR, Inc. His accountant has calculated that his stock, along with his other assets, will create an estate tax on his death of $150,000. Accordingly, PQR, Inc., has adopted an Internal Revenue Code 303 stock redemption plan, funding it with $150,000 of life insurance carrying a premium of $6,000 per year. PQR, Inc., is in a 50 percent tax bracket and has pretax earnings equal to 10 percent of sales.

An ESOT can provide the same liquidity for Mr. B's estate as an Internal Revenue Code 303 plan, at half the cost.

Annual Premium	Pretax Earnings Needed to Finance Through Section 303	Pretax Earnings Needed to Finance Through ESOT	Sales Needed:	Sales Needed to Finance Through Section 303	Sales Needed to Finance Through ESOT
$6,000	$12,000	$6,000		$120,000	$60,000

Fig. 3.7.   Case no. 7: Raising Cash
for a Major Stockholder

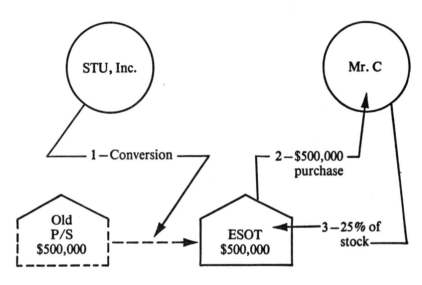

Mr. C owns 100 percent of STU, Inc. The company has sponsored a qualified profit-sharing plan for many years, and it presently has liquid securities worth $500,000. Mr. C's stock in STU, Inc., is valued at $2 million, and he would like to sell 25 percent of it to the profit-sharing plan for $500,000. The stock has never paid a dividend, and there are no prospects that it will.

Solution: Mr. C can sell 25 percent of his stock to the profit-sharing plan for $500,000, paying capital gains tax on the proceeds, by first converting the profit-sharing plan to an ESOP.

Mr. A, who owns 100 percent of the stock of MNO, Inc., is acquainted with a group of people who have offered to buy half his MNO stock for $500,000. Should he sell?

Solution: If an ESOT bought half of Mr. A's stock for $500,000 through an installment sale, he would still control 100 percent of the voting power of MNO, Inc.

FIG. 3.8.   CASE NO. 8: SALE OF BLOCK OF
CLOSELY HELD STOCK WHILE RETAINING CONTROL

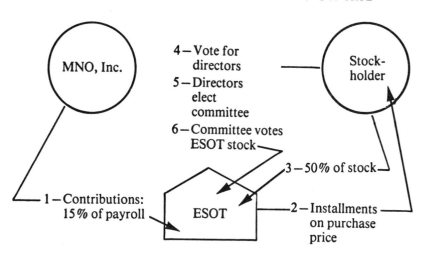

4

BANKER'S POINT OF VIEW, INCLUDING FIDUCIARY RESPONSIBILITIES

Family tax planning today requires the corporate stockholder-executive to review the ESOP as a full or partial solution to problems concerning estate planning. The ESOT is envisioned as a market for his stock through lifetime dispositions, i.e., an in-house market during the post-retirement period, or purchase may be made through the ESOT with deductible dollars, which lowers the after-tax cost of the acquisition. In the case of a lifetime disposition particularly, there is some likelihood that the company may have to be ruled out as a potential purchaser because of dividend problems arising on any redemption that does not qualify under IRS Section 302(b).

The banker's point of view takes on a new look when the financier realizes that funds accumulated in the trust prior to a redemption may be used as an ESOP financial tool. Also, an installment purchase agreement with future payments on the installment contract is useful to permit proper cash flow as well as long-term capital gains benefits.

Gene C. Albright, vice-president and executive trust officer of the Oregon Bank, sent the following internal correspondence to all officers of the bank—in the head office as well as the branches.

> The attached description of an employee benefit trust plan is unique. I bring it to your attention because it can be very effectively utilized to great advantage by some corporate entities.

48

Used properly, it works beautifully, but because of its unique advantages, I'm sure that some companies will try using it improperly as a "tax loophole." Its best and primary use should be for companies that have no financial problems, strong capital ratios, a history of consistently good quality earnings—and a desire to do something rewarding for their employees.

Many banks have taken the stance that they will not serve as trustee for such a trust—with no real basis for the conclusion other than "it's an untested trust with great potential liability." The Oregon Bank is not going to run afraid, we do have such a trust on the books now and we expect to accept appointments of future trusts like that described so long as they are properly structured and are given approval by the Internal Revenue Service, which must give special blessing on trusts which invest in stock of the corporate entity which makes the contribution.

This type of trust is particularly helpful to closely held corporations, where the owners do not have successor family management and desire a sale which does not hand back a fistful of another stock or a handful of tax problems to take in one year.

If you feel there are situations that might fit into the described trust arrangement, please call me.

Banks and other institutional lenders have key roles concerning the future of ESOP as a financial vehicle. Unless the lender realizes the importance of the ESOP's ability to generate twice the cash flow to amortize loans, less corporate cash will be retained. ESOP's favorable corporate tax laws enable the *inside* dollar to make loan payments—at twice the rate of outside dollars. The payment of principal and interest through the employee trust permits the pretax dollar deduction, which in turn lets company cash go twice the ordinary distance (see fig. 3.2).

Bankers understand that the cash-flow method rests on the time-honored maxim that "money begets money."[1] Dollars on hand today can be invested in profitable projects and thereby yield additional funds to the investing company. Funds to be received at a future date cannot be profitably invested until the date the dollars are received. Therefore, they have no earning power in the interim. For this reason, a corporate concern must place a time value on

---

1. John G. McLean, "How to Evaluate New Capital Investments," p. 324.

its money—a dollar in hand today is much more valuable than one
to be received at a future time.

Bankers are becoming increasingly aware of the government-
rescue operational vehicles, such as those conducted by the Economic Development Administration (EDA). This division of the
Department of Commerce on June 6, 1975, granted the city of
South Bend, Indiana, $5 million in EDA funds. Title 9 of the
Public Works and Economic Development Act provides that states
or communities threatened by high unemployment may be granted
funds for "any reasonable means" of effecting economic adjustment. Regional EDA administrators have been instructed to give
priority to innovative projects.

QUESTION: Why would banks and other financial lenders have
interest in dollar grants such as those afforded by EDA?

ANSWER: The interest rate that the bank would charge the
company would be independently determined over the EDA interest rate, thereby affording the bank its normal dollar ROI; in
addition the bank would have a safe-harbor security position regarding collateral and guarantees; finally, the cash-flow benefits
to the borrower would allow a healthy amortization scheduling of
the loan.

Requirements for the EDA grant necessitate that local banks
participate with the total loan; in the South Bend plan, the banks
were required to lend the company $2 million. The rate of interest
charged by the banks not only permits them a sound ROI but also
enables their security position to be strengthened, due to the EDA
participating agreements. In table 4.1 an econometric analysis
compares the cash flow required to amortize a 3-percent loan
financed with EDA participation, and of a conventional loan at 8
percent interest. The table shows that the cash flow with the EDA
participation increases the corporate cash by $1,771,138 and
allows the loan to be amortized in seven and one-half years rather
than the ten years, ten months required for conventional financing.
If the loan also utilizes an ESOT, the corporation tax bracket of
50 percent permits leveraging, improving the cash position in the
amount of the tax savings—$5 million.

The low interest cost made possible by EDA participation, in
combination with the government-supported tax benefits of the

TABLE 4.1. CASH FLOW REQUIRED TO RETIRE
A $5-MILLION LOAN WITH AND WITHOUT EDA PARTICIPATION
(YEARLY PAYMENTS OF $750,000, INCLUDING INTEREST)
EDA Participation—*3 Percent Interest*

	Yearly Payment	Interest	Principal	Balance Due
1 year	$ 750,000	$ 150,000	$ 600,000	$4,400,000
2	750,000	132,000	618,000	3,782,000
3	750,000	113,460	636,540	3,145,460
4	750,000	94,364	655,636	2,489,824
5	750,000	74,695	675,305	1,814,519
6	750,000	54,436	695,564	1,118,955
7	750,000	33,569	716,431	402,524
8–6 mo.	408,562	6,038	402,524	0
	$5,658,562	$ 658,562	$5,000,000	

Conventional Loan—*8 Percent Interest*

	Yearly Payment	Interest	Principal	Balance Due
1 year	$ 750,000	$ 400,000	$ 350,000	$4,650,000
2	750,000	372,000	378,000	4,272,000
3	750,000	341,760	408,240	3,863,760
4	750,000	309,100	440,900	3,422,860
5	750,000	273,828	476,172	2,946,688
6	750,000	235,735	514,265	2,432,423
7	750,000	194,594	555,406	1,887,017
8	750,000	150,161	599,839	1,277,178
9	750,000	102,174	647,826	629,352
10–10 mo.	679,700	50,348	629,352	0
	$7,429,700	$2,429,700	$5,000,000	

Pretax Annual Earnings Required

	Without ESOT	With ESOT	Cash Flow Savings
8% Conventional Financing	$12,429,700	$7,429,700	$5,000,000
3% EDA Participation	10,658,562	5,658,562	5,000,000
Difference =	$ 1,771,138	$1,771,138	

ESOP trust, i.e., writing off the loan interest and principal payments, generates an immediate changeover from a sick company to a healthy one.

As a result of using such a combination plan, South Bend Lathe, Inc., by November 1975, had prepaid over six months' debt payments to the city and banks; granted all employees a vacation bonus of a week's extra pay; and given all employees a $50.00 Christmas bonus and a pay increase that wasn't promised them until October 1976. Average pay to the employees was $5.75 per hour. Quite a contrast to Henry Ford's 1914 revolutionary pay raise to $5.00 per day!

The banks, which act as trustees, are naturally concerned with valuation procedures. Some banks insist on performing the valuation themselves, while other banks desire an outside appraisal that tests the appraisal of their own valuation department. In regard to an ESOT, it is important to make certain that the trust document carefully stipulate the valuation responsibilities. It should contain a provision that a professional independent appraiser initially determine the going-in value, and it should also stipulate a method of annually updating the stock computation. ERISA Regulation 403(a) (1) offers a guideline that will satisfy any trustee's obligation by assuring the bank that it is receiving proper directions under the regulations.

TRUSTEES' PERSPECTIVE AND
FIDUCIARY RESPONSIBILITIES

Section 401(a) (1) of ERISA sets forth general standards under which fiduciaries must be guided in the discharge of their duties. The fiduciary must act as follows:

(1) solely in the interest of planned participants and their beneficiaries and for the exclusive purpose of providing benefits to them, and

(2) with the care, skill, prudence and diligence under the circumstances then prevailing that a prudent man acting in a like capacity and familiar with such matters would use in the conduct of a similar enterprise, and

(3) by diversifying investments so as to minimize the risk of large losses, and finally

(4) in accordance with the plan documents insofar as they are consistent with ERISA Regulations.

ESOPs are specifically exempt from the diversification requirement in number (3) above. However, since they are not specifically exempt by ERISA from the general prudence requirement
under (2) above, the question has been raised as to whether a
trustee can safely acquire company stock and hold it under circumstances in which the acquisition or holdings may be deemed im-
prudent—for example, when the company's stock values decline.[2]

The writer's opinion is that the ESOT fiduciary is not subject
to the general prudence standard for the acquisition and holding
of company stock, as stated in number (2) of Section 401(a) (1)
above. Rather, the level of prudence for the trustee would be related directly to the purpose and design of the plan under which
he acts, and would therefore be measured by the skill and care of
other ESOT trustees acting in a like capacity. The trust instrument
is the important vehicle that protects the fiduciary's position and
thoroughly indicates the areas in which the trust and the trustees
shall operate. Obviously, if a trust or trustee were found guilty of
a breach of trust for not following the provisions of the plan, the
trust could be disqualified, and the trustee would have legal consequences to pay.

Members of the legal profession—especially those working with
trusts—know that the intent of trust law has been that a trustee
has the right to invest assets of the trust without liability concerning
the investment in a given security if the trustee follows the written
terms of the trust instrument that is designed for that purpose. The
fiduciary's responsibility includes the use of discretionary controls
over the management of the trust assets or the ESOP. As previously stated, the trust officer of the Oregon Bank emphasized in
his letter that only companies that have no financial problems and
possess strong capital ratios, a history of consistently good-quality
earnings, and a desire to do something rewarding for their employees should even consider an ESOP formation. By setting up
ESOPs only for this type of company, the fiduciary will remain
clearly within the laws relating to the bank's position of security
and the trust department's responsibility, as well as the laws governing the fiduciary and trustees themselves.

The voting power for an ESOP should be outlined in its trust

---

2. Ronald M. Bushman, "ESOPs: A Trustee's Perspective," *Trust and
Estate,* June 1976.

documents. Such documents generally outline the mechanics of trustee voting but give the plan committee appointed by management the authority to direct the trustees in voting shares of company stock that are owned by the trust. Management, in turn, is allowed to direct the plan committee's recommendations. The reason for such an arrangement is obvious: without this authority, the "tail would wag the dog." To maintain authority in a company, management's outside stock must be placed in a position to control the inside stock owned by the trust. Unless the outside stock has authority to direct sales and make company policy, there will be a split in management, which in this writer's view is a road of discord without direction. The trust instruments therefore must be designed so that the plan committee has the authority to direct the trustees in the voting of ESOP stock, thereby permitting management to manage. Each situation, however, should be considered individually; there should be a management audit review to make policy regarding controls, voting powers, types of stock to be issued, and other preliminary matters before major decisions are considered.

There may be a possible conflict of interest if a bank services the debt of a corporation and at the same time acts as trustee for that corporation's ESOP. Such situations must be carefully reviewed, and proper decisions made. If a bank acts as both lender and fiduciary for a plan, it may have to act to protect loan assets and enforce related contracts, while at the same time implementing its fiduciary duty to the ESOP. Ronald M. Bushman, in charge of the trust department of Redwood Bank, San Francisco, gave the following example regarding a possible conflict of interest.

> For example, should the employer company fall upon hard times, it may find it difficult or impossible to make its annual contributions to the trust, causing a default in the loan. The employees' interest might best be served by attempting to renegotiate the terms of the loan, while the bank's interest may best be served by enforcing its collateral and otherwise attempting to collect the loan. In an extreme case it might cause the company to collapse.

Because these and similar situations may arise, some banks are extremely cautious about accepting an ESOP in their trust department. The wisdom of the trust department in carefully reviewing the history of the company and its purpose is most important in determining acceptance of the fiduciary responsibility.

GENERAL RULES RELATING TO PROHIBITED TRANSACTIONS

As set forth in Section 406 of ERISA, the principal prohibited-transaction rules regarding the establishment of an employee benefit plan created or maintained to invest significantly in employer equity securities, i.e., an ESOP, are directed toward self-dealing between the plan and so-called disqualified persons. Disqualified persons comprise (1) the employer corporation sponsoring the plan; (2) any officer, director, or highly compensated employee of the employer corporation; and (3) certain relatives of a major shareholder of an employer corporation.

The reason for these prohibitions is obvious: to prevent people inside the company from seizing personal gain at the cost of employees who own stock through a qualified plan. Obviously, the prohibited-transaction ruling is a safeguard for all participants who share in the employee trust. Section 409 of ERISA clearly defines the fiduciary's responsibility in this regard, and it holds the fiduciary accountable for any losses sustained by the plan that result from the fiduciary's failure to enforce the prohibitions. In many instances, a plan has only one trustee, because this is the most expedient way to deal with methods of allocation of stock in debt, accounting considerations, security act problems, and general unrelated business-income problems. An officer of the employer company may serve as such a plan trustee without violating the laws of ERISA. On the other hand, if a fiduciary fails to properly discharge his basic fiduciary responsibilities as set forth in Section 404 of ERISA, or permits the plan to engage in a prohibited transaction as described in Section 406 of ERISA or if the transaction involves other self-dealings, the fiduciary then has placed himself in a problem position. The fiduciary can protect himself by engaging an attorney who is not associated with the company or the bank to assist with and/or pass judgment on committee activity. Because of this participation, these activities may be viewed as arm's-length transactions. It is wise to receive a letter at least once a year from this outside attorney mentioning the fact that he assisted the committee on some of its decisions and to retain this item for future purposes.

Experienced and competent professionals who are students of trust regulations and accountability should be used in forming the plan and trust for an ESOP. Properly designed and organized, the ESOP will provide unusual flexibility and rewards to the company, its shareholders, and its employees.

The transactions described below, which would normally be prohibited transactions, are permitted by ERISA when they are undertaken by an ESOT:

1. The sale of stock by a disqualified person to a qualified trust even at a fair price is normally a prohibited transaction. This is specifically authorized, however, when an ESOT is the buyer. IRC Sec. 4975(d) (13) and ERISA Sec. 408(e).

2. A loan to a qualified trust by a disqualified person is normally a prohibited transaction. But IRC Sec. 4975(d) (13) specifically exempts a loan made to an ESOT if such loan is collateralized only by "employer securities" and is for the exclusive benefit of plan participants.

3. Current literature regarding ESOTs frequently describes transactions in which a loan is made to the ESOT by a bank or other financial institution, the loan being guaranteed by the employer company. This form of financing is acceptable and encouraged by the Conference Committee Report.

In the absence of the exemptive provision of ERISA's Section 407(b)(1) in conjunction with Section 407(d)(3), the transactions described below would be prohibited. However, at least one of them is likely to occur in connection with the formation of an ESOP in order to purchase a block of employer stock.

1. The sale or exchange of property between the plan and a "disqualified person" (or "party in interest")

2. The transfer of plan assets to, or for the benefit of, a "disqualified person" (or "party in interest")

3. The act of a "fiduciary" whereby he deals with plan assets in his own interest

4. The lending of money or other extension of credit (e.g., a loan guarantee) between the plan and a "disqualified person" (or "party in interest")

However, as previously mentioned, ERISA has the effect of exempting a profit-sharing, stock-bonus, or "employee stock ownership" plan from the restrictions of Section 407(a) as long as the plan specifies a maximum percentage of asset value that may be invested in employer stock.

Sections of ERISA and the Internal Revenue Code exempt from the prohibited-transaction rules of Section 406 and 4975(c) the acquisition or sale by any pension-benefit plan of "qualifying employer securities" (defined in Section 407(d)(5) or ERISA to include stock of the employer corporation), provided—

1. no commission is charged on the transaction;
2. the acquisition of the stock is compatible with the limitations of Section 407 of ERISA; and
3. the acquisition (or sale) is for "adequate consideration," which means the public market price in the case of "a security for which there is a generally recognized market" or, if there is no such market, the "fair market value" as determined in good faith by the trustee or other plan "fiduciary" in accordance with regulations of the secretary of labor.[3]

---

3. James G. Phillipp, ed., *Fiduciary Responsibility*, pp. 353–57.

5

VALUING STOCK

IN THE

SMALL- TO MEDIUM-SIZED

CLOSELY HELD

CORPORATION

An in-depth study of the rationale behind the method of valuing stock in closely held corporations will assist CEOs, presidents, owner-managers, and finance officers in corporate planning and compliance with government regulations. Small and medium-sized firms find it difficult to establish fair market value for their corporate stock as required under Internal Revenue Ruling 59-60. Such troubles will lessen to the degree the company designs, organizes, and develops written procedures for its stock-valuing operation.

Advantages derived from annual valuation of closely held stock include: improving the company's in-house and public image, acquiring new money for short- and long-term capital needs, and attracting innovative and productive company executives.

Closely held corporations are rapidly becoming a dying species —dying because they don't know how to value and leverage the assets they have.

Most closely held companies do not realize that these assets are highly valuable when there is a planned perpetuity in management. This can be organized by valuing the company and sharing part of the stock ownership with the management that will provide perpetuity.

It is important to ascertain the minority stockholders' interest in the common equity securities, since doing so represents the arm's-length transactions that involve the willing buyer/willing seller fairness necessary to ratiocinate values. Most security valuations for determining stock values encompass factors set forth in Revenue Ruling 59-60. The following components should be analyzed for valuations of closely held stock:

1. Nature of the business and history of the enterprise from its inception
2. Economic outlook in general and condition and outlook of the specific industry in particular
3. Book value of the stock and financial condition of the business
4. Earnings capacity of the company
5. Dividend-paying capacity
6. Whether or not the enterprise has goodwill or other intangible value
7. Sales of the stock and size of block to be valued
8. Market price of stocks of corporations engaged in the same or a similar line of business having their stocks actively traded in a free and open market, either on an exchange or over the counter

Also, in order to reach sound conclusions as to fair market value of the stock, consideration should be given to the following:

1. The company's management and going-concern status
2. Company facilities and capacity (refer to Data Resources forecast of the U.S. economy—billions of dollars table)
3. The company's current and historical financial condition and an analysis of its assets and capital structure
4. Current and historical net worth
5. Projected earnings for the near and immediate terms

Revenue Ruling 59-60, covering the valuation of stocks and bonds for estate and gift tax purposes, quotes the regulations as defining fair market value:

> as the price at which the property would change hands between a willing buyer and a willing seller when the former is not under any compulsion to buy and the latter is not under any compulsion to sell, both parties having reasonable knowledge of the relevant factor.

The following data illustrate the management strategy needed concerning the in-depth management audit analysis. The valuation formulas should include sufficient mathematical back-up work to endure a stockholder's challenge or an IRS audit.

HISTORY AND NATURE OF THE BUSINESS

It is pertinent to review the history and nature of the business to determine its past stability or instability, its growth or lack of growth, the diversity or lack of diversity of its operations, and other factors needed to form an opinion of the degree of risk involved in the business.

History

The history to be studied should include, but need not be limited to, the business's products or services, its marketing area and system, its affiliated or subsidiary companies, and a description of company ownership and employee relationships. This information is obtained through company records and interviews with key management personnel.

Company Facilities

A description of the company's operating facilities, i.e., land, buildings and equipment, is included in the performance audit. The locations, age, state of repair, and capacity of the facilities all have an impact on the future earning capability of the company. Plant location is important because transportation costs are often a significant expense item for both product- and service-oriented firms.

In addition, environmental regulations and restrictions can directly affect the company's capabilities at a given location. In the case of a manufacturing company, the physical condition of the company's facilities can directly affect its ability to meet market demand for its products.

Estimating the firm's capacity is important because, if capacity is reached in a period of high demand for the company's services and management has not made alternative production plans, the company will lose available sales dollars. Assessors' records, i.e., county property tax statements, are checked for property valuation, and, if warranted, a valuation by a certified property and/or equipment appraiser is acquired.

Operational Audit

A review of company management is a vital part of the measurement of the risk class associated with the business. Why do some companies in the same industry have better growth records than others? Sometimes it is because they enjoy an unduplicated characteristic, such as a unique geographic location or a special service/production process. More often, however, it is because they are better managed.

Modern management audits reveal that good managers will be effective in almost any company. This is because they are masters, not of a particular business, but rather of critical managerial functions: setting objectives, formulating plans to achieve those objectives, organizing and inspiring subordinates to carry out plans, and innovating when previous methods seem outmoded. Thus, a thorough analysis of a company's growth prospects must go beyond the quantitative approach. It must take into account the quality of management.

During the valuation process, interviews are held with key managerial personnel in order to gain insight into their concept of the company's market, their ability to delegate authority and responsibility, and their strategies and desire for growth. The management section of the valuation report includes a list of the company's management team including a description of each individual, his job title and responsibilities, age, education, job experience, and compensation.

It is important to review these items in order to equate job skill and responsibility with adequate compensation. If this equality does not exist, adjustments can be made in order to restate company expense to better reflect proper salary levels.

ECONOMIC CONDITIONS

A sound appraisal of the closely held company must consider current and prospective economic conditions in the national and local economy, as well as in the industries with which the company does business. Trends and conditions in the national economy have a significant impact on the risk class of the business. They affect the company's cost of borrowing and ability to borrow, the required rate of return on investment, and the spending patterns of the industry and the public sector. Current and long-term economic projections are obtainable from forecasts made by the Economic Research Department of the U.S. Department of Commerce, and from econometric exhibits constructed by Data Resources, Inc. Local economic information is acquired primarily from publications produced by various state and municipal sources.

Considerations relevant to the microeconomics of the firm include the sources and availability of raw materials, the competitive status of the firm in the market, and other competitive factors. It is important to know the status of the company in the industry and whether it is maintaining a stable position with respect to competitors.

FINANCIAL INFORMATION

An in-depth review of the financial condition of the company is essential in the valuation process. Financial information for at least a five-year period is thoroughly analyzed. Trends and growth rates in gross sales and profitability are investigated, and the capital structure of the business is analyzed. A ratio analysis is completed that depicts trends in liquidity, solvency, leverage, and capital adequacy.

Valuations offer other advantages that have been promulgated by tax regulations. Recently Congress has made it possible for the valuation of the closely held corporation to include trust ownership of "key-man" life insurance to buy out the closely held corporate stockholder (a financial vehicle that allows bankers to participate in the stock valuation process). Funding of the buyout is a necessary component in determining methodology of the stock valuation.

Table 5.1 is a typical analysis of financial data for a sample company.

Ratio Analysis

In order to further investigate the financial condition of the company, a ratio analysis of the company is shown in table 5.2.

As is evident from a review of the current and quick ratios, the company has a strong working capital position and adequate liquidity and solvency. The major reason for the significant increase in 1976 and 1977 was a change in the accounting procedure

TABLE 5.1. ANALYSIS OF FINANCIAL DATA
FOR A SAMPLE COMPANY

The growth factors pertaining to total assets are important when structuring a company's stock worth. The figures shown in table 5.1 reveal an average annual increase of $8.8 million for fiscal years 1973–77. This $35+ million addition to starting assets represents a 190-percent increase for the period and a compound growth rate of 20.59 percent. Net income increased over $1.5 million, or 629 percent. The substantial gain in company earnings for the two years 1976 and 1977 enabled the stockholders to increase stockholder dividends $.15 per share. The dividend payout ratio was raised during 1977 to reflect the 1976–77 profit picture.

Total Assets	Net Worth	Gross Sales	Net Income	Net Income P/S*	Fiscal Year
$31,750,050	$5,672,046	$ 8,655,310	$ 249,588	$ .09	1973
38,275,011	5,937,360	13,165,282	421,803	.16	1974
49,580,233	6,668,384	16,920,405	1,201,312	.46	1975
57,301,366	7,975,212	20,215,333	1,677,845	.65	1976
66,875,216	9,425,464	22,633,804	1,819,364	.70	1977

*2,575,350 shares o/s

TABLE 5.2. RATIO ANALYSIS

	1973	1974	1975	1976	1977
Current Ratio	1.87	1.96	1.93	5.79	4.02
Quick Ratio	1.56	1.49	1.52	4.52	3.17
Debt/Worth	4.80	6.15	6.97	6.63	6.40
Return on Net Worth	4.40	7.10	18.01	21.04	19.30
Bank Debt/Net Worth	2.08	3.05	3.46	3.32	3.48

used to report notes payable. The remaining ratios indicate the highly leveraged position of the company. Debt to worth has averaged 6.5 to 1 over the past three years.

According to trend, the debt/worth ratio will finally approach 10 to 1 by 1983. As net worth and profitability increase over the years, bank debt will grow even faster. If the company does indeed continue to rely on debt for growth, then growth will be directly affected by the company's ability to obtain financing and may be undercapitalized at some time in the future.

Valuation

There are six commonly used methods of valuing closely held stock. These are:

1. Book value
2. Adjusted book value
3. Liquidation value
4. Capitalization of current or average earnings
5. Discounted future earnings
6. Comparable publicly held companies

Book Value   Generally speaking, book value, or net worth, is a fair representation of the value of the underlying assets only in cases where most assets are liquid in nature and therefore more closely reflect their current market value. Possible exceptions to this are companies that do not take accelerated depreciation or are constantly adding to their fixed assets so that depreciated book value .is not widely divergent from fair market value.

Adjusted Book Value   When book value is not felt to represent accurately the current fair market value of underlying assets and liabilities, it is necessary to adjust this figure for known variances between book value and fair market value and other possible contingencies.

Liquidation Value   This method of valuation is a departure from valuing the business on a going-concern basis. It assumes the business ceases operation and sells off all assets and pays its liabilities. That which is left over would go to the owners. This calculation is meaningful only to indicate an absolute bottom price for the company, below which an owner would be better off to liquidate rather than sell (this ignores obligations to employees, customers, etc.).

Capitalization of Earnings   The real value of any business concern, when approached on a return on investment basis, is in its earning power. An owner cannot enjoy the book value or liquidated value unless the assets are sold, which is undesirable because then the business would cease to exist.

Several variations of earnings value are possible. An average of four or five earnings could be used, as an example. Current earnings or a weighted average of past earnings are also possibilities. The main premise is that past or current earnings are an indication of future earnings and can therefore be used to value the firm. Through the Revenue Ruling 59-60 approach to weighted average of the past year or years, normal operations are calculated to determine valuation.

Discounted Future Earnings   As mentioned above, the most important thing to an owner of a business is setting a value regarding earnings. Future earnings should be emphasized since past earnings are no longer available to the owner. In order to estimate future earnings, many things must be taken into account, including the past and present growth rate of the firm. With this growth rate established, earnings can be projected for some period in the future and then discounted back to the present to establish the present value of those future earnings. Five-year projected earnings—net aftertax earnings—are utilized in the analysis. Your firm's controller or presentative accountant assists in the projections since they are annually preparing pro forma information for management regarding sales, cash flow, and net earnings.

Comparable Publicly Held Companies   In some cases it is possible to find one or more publicly traded companies comparable enough in nature and size to apply their earnings multiple to the closely held company. This is rarely the case, simply because most publicly held companies are much larger and more diverse in their operations and have a more complex capital structure.

OVERVIEW AND APPRAISAL

The final section of the report is valuation and appraisal strategy. Here, various factors that affect the value of the firm are quantified. Based on information gathered on the company, its management, competition, current and forecasted economic conditions, and historical operating performance, projections are established for the future of the company. In analyzing various approaches to valuing the business, emphasis is placed on the method thought most representative of the fair market value of the company.

In regard to the sample business, it is thought that emphasis should be placed on projecting future earnings and applying an appropriate discount rate to arrive at a present value.

Total sales have been projected for a five-year period using three bisociated assumptions, as shown in table 5.3.

Assumption 1 Sales will grow at a rate equivalent to the projected growth rate for GNP over the next five years and then level off in perpetuity.

This assumption considers uncertainties about the general economy and the possible effect of the company's inability to maintain capital base adequate to sustain growth.

Assumption 2 Sales will grow for two years at a rate equivalent to the trend based on an analysis of the last five years plus the projected growth rate in GNP. Sales will return to the historical 1975–77 growth rate of 15.7 percent for the following three years and then level off in perpetuity.

This assumption considers the fact that interest expense has a significant impact on the company's profitability, and, in the light of developments in the economy that have direct effect on the level of interest rates, the trend in total sales should perhaps be adjusted to reflect these factors. Long-term econometric forecasts prepared by Data Resources, Inc., predicted that the level of economic growth would return to historical growth rates by late 1978 or early 1979, but 1980 disproved this forecast as inflation pushed the prime rate to record highs. Since interest rates are not receding as hoped, companies should establish industry projections while taking into account the cost of money for the next three to five years.

Assumption 3 For the next five years (1978–82), sales will continue to grow at a rate equivalent to the most recent five-year annual compound growth rate; then sales will level off in perpetuity.

This assumption is based on the company's historical performance vis-à-vis the economy. It takes into account the company's reputation in the marketplace and its unique organizational structure which will enable it to maintain the historical growth rate.

TABLE 5.3. PROJECTED EARNINGS—
THREE BISOCIATED TECHNIQUES

	Assumption 1	Assumption 2	Assumption 3
1978	$1,972,277	$1,995,842	$2,193,971
1979	2,129,487	2,261,289	2,645,709
1980	2,299,288	2,616,311	3,190,460
1981	2,482,559	3,027,071	3,847,375
1982	2,680,444	3,502,321	4,639,549

In light of the return available on other investments, the prevailing capitalization rates in the financial market, and based on information gathered on the company management, competition, and historical operating performance, an 18 percent discount rate is considered appropriate. A discounted future earnings value is calculated as follows: from the sales projections, net aftertax earnings have been extrapolated at the average historical margin of 7.9 percent of sales.

In light of recent developments in the economy and the historical operating performance of the company, the following subjective probabilities were assigned to each bisociated assumption:

Assumption 1—10 percent
Assumption 2—10 percent
Assumption 3—80 percent

If earnings are projected out five years and then assumed to level off in perpetuity, they must then be discounted back to the present to determine present value. In the application of this

TABLE 5.4. DETERMINING PERCENT VALUE
USING THREE MATHEMATICAL ASSUMPTIONS

Year	Projected Income	Present Value Factor	Present Value
Assumption 1 (10% probability)			
1978	$1,972,277	.847	$1,670,519
1979	2,129,487	.718	1,528,972
1980	2,299,288	.609	1,400,266
1981	2,482,559	.516	1,281,000
1982	2,680,444	.437	1,171,354
1982 + 2,680,444 × 100/18 = 14,891,356		.437	6,507,522
		Present Value	$13,559,633
Assumption 2 (10% probability)			
1978	$1,995,842	.847	$1,690,478
1979	2,261,289	.718	1,623,606
1980	2,616,311	.609	1,593,333
1981	3,027,071	.516	1,561,969
1982	3,502,321	.437	1,530,514
1982 + 3,502,321 × 100/18 = 19,457,339		.437	8,502,857
		Present Value	$16,502,757
Assumption 3 (80% probability)			
1978	$2,193,971	.847	$1,858,293
1979	2,645,709	.718	1,899,619
1980	3,190,460	.609	1,942,990
1981	3,847,375	.516	1,985,246
1982	4,639,549	.437	2,027,483
1982 + 4,639,549 × 100/18 = 25,775,272		.437	11,263,793
		Present Value	$20,977,424
	Assumption 1	$13,559,633 × .10 =	$ 1,355,963
	Assumption 2	16,502,757 × .10 =	1,650,275
	Assumption 3	20,977,424 × .80 =	16,781,939
		TOTAL VALUE	$19,788,177

method, it is necessary to choose an appropriate discount rate. Among the more important factors to be taken into consideration are:

1. Nature of the business
2. Stability and trend of earnings
3. Alternative investments available

The company's stock is not traded on an exchange of any kind, and the appraised value must be discounted to make allowance for this nonmarketability factor. When determining an appropriate discount for lack of marketability, various factors are taken into consideration, such as the cost of flotation of industrial common stocks and the implicit costs of making a public market in an unseasoned security.

With a 10 percent discount for nonmarketability, the total appraised value is: $19,788,177 $\times$ .90 = $17,809,359, according to calculations shown in table 5.4.

In the final analysis, without having a meaningful market value report, it is highly unlikely anyone would be interested in acquiring or perpetuating a closely held corporation.

6

PRELIMINARY

FEASIBILITY ANALYSIS:

DESIGN CONSIDERATIONS

An in-depth survey of a company, prior to making financial commitments, is necessary in order to determine feasibility of the ESOP design. For the company to maximize the leveraging and deferred-compensation benefits, financial managers and advisers should thoroughly investigate whether the following potential uses of an ESOP are desired and how best to implement them. (See table A.1, "General Corporate Information.")

1. Distribute ownership of company among employees to reward long service
2. Encourage employee concern with company progress toward increased efficiency and productivity
3. Create a market for the sale of company stock
4. Obtain new financing, using pretax dollars
5. Refinance existing company debt, using pretax dollars
6. Finance acquisitions with pretax dollars
7. Create a market for the purchase of a subsidiary or division
8. Finance a tender offer for the repurchase of company stock

The company seeking a financial design including plan objectives should presently be operating profitably, thereby paying taxes in a full corporate position. Current profitability, however, is not absolutely requisite for utilizing leverage benefits of the financial plan. Determining eligibility requires a management analysis study in order that professionally, the team, i.e., the company's legal and accounting representatives, can prepare alternatives, electives, and the time-and-sequence schedule.

In all likelihood, an ESOP will favorably motivate employees more than other types of deferred compensation plans, since an ESOP—in substance—gives the company employees a "piece of the action" via ownership of company stock. The plan gives employees a direct and vested interest in the success of their company, thereby establishing an identity of interest between management and labor.

The following remarks, charts, and graphic illustrations concern an actual case in progress; they illustrate the preliminary procedures for conducting a management analysis study for "Mr. A. B. Smith, President, U.S.A. Profit Co., Inc., Anytown, U.S.A."

BACKGROUND INFORMATION

Mr. A. B. Smith, President
U.S.A. Profit Co., Inc.
Anytown, U.S.A.

Dear Mr. Smith:

The purpose of this agreement is to set forth the terms of our proposal for the formation and organization of, and to assist you with the implementation of a financial plan that will include an employee stock ownership plan for U.S.A. Profit Co., Inc.

The main objectives of the use of a financial plan for U.S.A. Profit Co., Inc. (the Company), as we understand them are as follows:

1. To provide a financial plan whereby the Company can use pretax dollars to retire present and future long-term debt; pay off the balance due on treasury stock with pretax deductions instead of using aftertax retained earnings; erect a new warehouse, and provide a financial method of acquiring new store outlets whereby the Company operation can best leverage sales, cost of sales, and the dollars spent for operational purposes.

2. To provide a means by which the Company may increase cash flow and finance its continuous growth, i.e., leverage

the combined federal and state corporate tax for growth purposes.

3. To provide a means whereby the employees of the Company will be able to acquire minimal stock ownership in the Company, so that employees will have a direct interest in the success of the business.

4. To provide an in-house market for the future acquisition of Company stock from existing shareholders, using pretax dollars.

5. To provide for additional employee incentive and motivation, and to provide for their future retirement security, meanwhile giving employees a real incentive to remain with the Company, and to provide a means of attracting new employees who have valuable knowledge and skills.

The background facts as we understand them are as follows:

1. The U.S.A. Profit Co., Inc., incorporated April 1, 1968, at Anytown, U.S.A., by authorizing 500 shares of common stock. Presently, there are 300 shares issued to A. B. Smith, President, and 200 shares are unissued.

2. The Company is engaged in the business of buying and selling merchandise and recently has moved into its new, modern store located at Anytown, U.S.A.

3. Presently, credit sales are being financed through the General Electric Credit Corporation, and, if negotiations were made to buy back the accounts currently, it would require approximately $750,000 to transact this business.

4. The Company has been and is profitable. Pretax profit in fiscal year ending March 31, 1975, of $82,426 was generated from sales of $2,386,298. Presently, the Company for the nine months ending December 31, 1975, records sales of $2,934,120, with pretax profits of $131,412. The Company, however, expects for fiscal year ending March 31, 1976, that the pretax earnings will level at approximately $150,000. It is important to note that approximately $30,000 has been expended during this fiscal year for moving from one location to another, including unusual and abnormal rents and other costs.

5. The Company's payroll is currently in excess of $435,000 nonunion payroll, and the projection for the future is that payroll will increase at approximately 10 percent annually to account for inflation and the hiring of additional employees as a result of increased sales.

6. The Company has a cash profit-sharing bonus plan with no accumulated assets, since annually the bonus is paid directly to the employees. The plan has been successful, and $28,786 was paid out for fiscal year ending March 31, 1974; $65,961 for fiscal year ending March 31, 1975; for current nine-month financial statement with projections for fiscal year March 31, 1976, $56,000.

7. Table 6.1 is a pro forma analysis of projected pretax earnings, net profit after tax, executive salary compensation, and covered payroll for the five-year period ending March 31, 1980.

VALUATION OF U.S.A. PROFIT CO., INC.

The following valuation approach to the U.S.A. Profit Co., Inc., stock values is being illustrated on a pro forma method of approach as it relates to the pretax earnings shown. It is important to keep in mind that we can ascertain an arm's length approach to annually establishing the value of the Company stock only through a qualified appraisal company that will endeavor to establish what would be paid by a rational buyer having knowledge of the prices of similar securities of similar companies and many other relevant factors. This approach would ensure the willing buyer/willing seller concept of fair market value.

Pro Forma Stock Valuation

The market for closely held corporation stock is limited. All the issued shares of U.S.A. Profit Co., Inc., are held by one shareholder, Mr. A. B. Smith (300 shares common stock. An additional 200 shares are unissued). Therefore, the elements of a *fair market* are limited. A fair market has been defined as follows:

A market created by buyers willing to buy and sellers willing to sell—where offers to sell challenge the attention of buyers and offers to buy challenge the attention of sellers.

[*Walter* v. *Duffy*, 387 F. 41, 46 (3rd Cir. 1923)]

TABLE 6.1　PRO FORMA ANALYSIS

Year	Projected Sales (M = thousands)	(1) Estimated Profit before Tax	(2) Net Profit after Tax*
1　(3-31-76)	(a)　$3,800 M	$150,000	$ 82,500
2　(3-31-77)	(b)　4,200 M	300,956	165,525
3　(3-31-78)	(c)　5,000 M	325,000	178,750
4　(3-31-79)	(d)　5,350 M	347,750	191,262
5　(3-31-80)	(e)　5,750 M	373,750	205,563

	(3) Executive Payroll	Amount % of Total	(4) Other Salaries	Amount % of Total	(5) Total Covered Compensation
(a)	$135,600	31.173	$299,400	68.827	$435,000
(b)	157,700	33.914	307,300	66.086	465,000
(c)	168,200	33.640	331,800	66.360	500,000
(d)	179,500	33.240	360,500	66.760	540,000
(e)	194,500	33.534	385,500	66.466	580,000

*Computed at current combined Federal and State Corporate rates

There are a number of ways to value stock in a closely held corporation. These approaches include valuation based on—

1. a capitalization of adjusted earnings;
2. an adjusted book value approach;
3. values of "comparable" corporations that are actively traded; and
4. values based on customary ways of valuing a business of your type.

As a practical matter, the two basic approaches used by the IRS in valuing most closely held corporations are:
1. A capitalization of adjusted earnings;
2. An adjusted book value approach.

The problem with a valuation based on a "comparable" corporation (which is actively traded) is that, for most closely held corporations, such as U.S.A. Profit Co., Inc., there are no exact "comparables." A publicly traded corporation often has more management depth, a longer growth record, a more-diversified capital structure, broader markets and greater market control, a history of paying dividends, an established position in its industry, a larger line of credit, and readily saleable stock. In addition, the value of the stock in a publicly traded corporation is subject to speculative pressure, which often produces unrealistic price/earnings ratios.

IRS Regulations list a number of economic factors, ranging from a company's position in an industry to the quality of its management, that should be considered in valuing a closely held corporation (*Reg. 20.2031-2[F]*). The economic factors mentioned in the Regulations are important when trying to establish an estate's right to a discount. The estate often tries using a capitalization of adjusted earnings or an adjusted book value approach. These factors are also important if the case is to be tried before the tax court, U.S. district court, or the court of claims. It should be noted that—

> I.R.S. tends to rely on rules of thumb for initial valuation.
> Careful studies are not made until the case is to be tried.
> [*Small Business Administration
> Market Research Summary No. 124, April, 1963*]

Let's examine the value of U.S.A. Profit Co., Inc., based on the two approaches used by the IRS in most cases: the adjusted book value approach and the adjusted capitalized earnings approach. This valuation is partially based on pro forma information that you have provided us, and the results are necessarily based on the quality of this information. We are sure you are interested in the results of the valuation process. However, it is equally important that you understand the approach used by the IRS and the reasons for any adjustments. Consequently, we will explain the approach and reasons for each adjustment. The valuation process is based on the Regulations, Revenue Rulings, cases, and experience of an IRS agent who has worked in the Estate and Gift Tax Division of the Internal Revenue Service.

Adjusted Book Value Approach

The first step in arriving at an adjusted book value is to examine the most recent balance sheet of U.S.A. Profit Co., Inc. (Refer to Company's Controller's December 31, 1975, financial statements.) The objective is to adjust the value of the assets shown on the balance sheet to their fair market value (*Rev. Rul. 59-60, 4.02[c] 1959-1 CB 237*).

Ten totally different adjustments are made, including asset fair market value, securities, inventory, reserves, loans, treasury stock, and other assets. In our illustration, we have included only those adjustments that have had an effect on your valuation.

1. *Shareholder's Equity* as shown on balance sheet, December 31, 1975.

   $252,165

2. + *Fair Market Value* of land and buildings over that shown on balance sheet.* (This value is based on the tax assessor's estimate of present fair market value based on comparable sales of similar property, and on your estimate of fair market value.)

   Note: Management Audit will contain a Tax Assessor's valuation as compared to present balance sheet listing.

3. + *Value of Goodwill.* (Goodwill is an intangible asset that may not be reflected on the balance sheet. In the final analysis, it is based on the company's earning capacity. [*Rev. Ruling 59-60, 4.02 (F) 1959-1 CB 237* as modified *Rev. Rul. 65-193, 1965-2 CB 370, Rev. Rul. 68-609, 1968-2 CB 237.*])

   $606,895

4. *Goodwill Computation*
   Earnings for Common Stock (refer to Item 8—Succeeding).

   $146,595

   a. Net Worth for Common Stock Adjusted (items 1 + 2, reduced by nonoperating assets). Note: The income from nonoperating assets

is *not* included in adjusted
aftertax income. We are concerned
here with an "excess" return
on operating assets. $252,165

b. Fair Rate of Return on Equity (for
your business). (A 10% rate of
return is often used when you cannot
establish to the satisfaction of the
IRS agent that a business of your
type usually earns more than 10%
return on capital equity.) $25,216

c. Adjusted Earnings for Common
Stock (see item 8 under
"Adjusted Capitalized Earnings"). $146,595

d. Fair Rate of Return on Equity. $25,216

e. Excess Earnings. $121,379

f. Excess Earnings Capitalized =
Goodwill. (The capitalization rate
used for this study is 5.) $606,895

5. *Adjusted Book Value*
a. Adjusted Net Worth
for Common Stock. $252,165

b. + Value of Goodwill, if any.   606,895
                                        _____

                                                           $859,060

*For this valuation, land and buildings are considered as having value shown
on company balance sheet.

Adjusted Capitalized Earnings

Often the real value of a business is in its ability to earn money.
One of the greatest jurists, Learned Hand, considered the issue of
valuation and concluded:

> Everyone knows that the shares in a commercial or manufac-
> turing company are chiefly dependent on what it will earn.
> [*Borg* v. *International Silver Company*, 11 F2d 147, 152 (1925)]

As a practical matter, the IRS agent usually capitalizes adjusted
earnings and compares this value to the U.S.A. Profit Co., Inc.,

	1976 (Year 1)	1977 (Year 2)	1978 (Year 3)	1979 (Year 4)	1980 (Year 5)
1. Net Income before Tax (As shown on P/L statement plus pro forma 1976–77)	$150,000	$300,956	$325,000	$347,750	$373,750
2. + Salaries over that which would have to be paid to key officers-stockholders by willing buyer." (Salaries of key shareholder officers are closely examined by the IRS. The test is not a reasonable salary for services actually rendered (*162 IRC*). The test is what a "willing buyer" who purchases stock in the business would have to pay to hire a manager with the same ability who is willing to devote the same amount of time to the business as the officer-stockholder does.	none	none	none	none	none
	For this management audit, the salary and bonus paid A. B. Smith are considered reasonable and fair.				
3. Adjusted Earnings before Tax	$150,000	$300,956	$325,000	$347,750	$373,750
4. Federal & State Corporate Tax	(67,500)	(135,431)	(146,250)	(156,488)	(168,187)
5. Adjusted Net Income after Tax	82,500	165,525	178,750	191,262	205,563
6. Trend of Adjusted Earnings for your Business	Variable Upward—Pretax earnings nearly doubled over the prior year period.				

7. **Year or Years to be Capitalized**
Should the trend of adjusted earnings for your business be cyclical, then the IRS usually capitalizes on the average of 5 years' adjusted earnings. However, if the trend is all up or all down, the IRS usually capitalizes only the most recent year's earnings, as they are the best measure of the value of the present earning power of your business.

8. **Actual Adjustment of Earnings**

Weighted

$$\begin{array}{rcl}
\$\ 82,500 \times 5 &=& \$412,500 \\
165,525 \times 4 &=& 662,100 \\
178,750 \times 3 &=& 536,250 \\
191,262 \times 2 &=& 382,524 \\
205,563 \times 1 &=& 205,563 \\
\hline
&& \$2,198,937 \\
&& \div\ 15 \\
&=& \$146,595
\end{array}$$

9. **Capitalization of Adjusted Earnings**
The capitalization factor used for this study is 5. This factor is often used by the IRS. A different capitalization factor may be warranted if your business is an extremely high risk or low risk business (see table 6.2).

$$5 \times \$146,595 = \$732,975$$

adjusted book value. The IRS agent will normally use the method that produces the highest value per share. The capitalization rate used is directly related to a rate of return on capital. The rate of return on capital varies with the risk, as shown in table 6.2.

TABLE 6.2.   RISK AND CAPITALIZATION RATE

	Rate of Return on Capital	Capitalization Factor
Low Risk	8%	12.5 times
Medium Risk	10%	10.0 times
High Risk	15%	6.6 times

Most businesses fall into the medium risk category. Consequently, most IRS agents figure capitalization at five to ten times adjusted earnings. For the purpose of this study, we have used the capitalization factor of five times adjusted earnings.

Earnings are adjusted in order to reflect the correct earning power of a business; adjustments are made in an effort to compensate for factors that tend to distort the earning power of a business. Profit-and-loss statements for a five-year period are used to determine whether there is a cyclical pattern to the earnings of a business. The average adjusted aftertax earnings for five years are capitalized if a cyclical pattern of earnings is evident. Greater weight is given to those years that more nearly reflect the corporation's future earnings potential if a cyclical earnings pattern is not evident. Only the last year is capitalized if the trend in earnings is all up or all down. In such a case, the most recent year more nearly reflects the current value of a company's earning power, and its future earnings potential. The point of all this is to determine a corporation's earning power based on its past performance (*Rev. Rul. 59-60, 4.02 (D), 1959-1 CB 237*). There are several other adjustments that also have to be made in computing the adjusted book value, including salaries, bonuses, rental payments, nonrecurring expenses, qualified plan contributions, stockholder loans, nonoperating assets, depreciation, etc. Our study includes only the adjustments pertinent to your firm.

Pages 78–79 show our adjustments to your profit and loss statements, based on five pro forma years via 1976–77 projections.

(Refer to Statement of Estimated Earnings, fiscal year ending March 31, 1976.)

Comparison Process

The IRS normally compares the adjusted book value and adjusted capitalized earnings and selects the higher of the two values. It is also important to note that the family partnership 6 percent fee charges would have to be considered in an IRS valuation (*Rev. Rul. 59-60*).

1.	Value based on adjusted book value	$859,060
2.	Value based on adjusted capitalized earnings	$732,975
3.	Higher value	$859,060

This is an estimate of the fair market value of your business, i.e., pro forma analysis based on techniques that are often used by the IRS. No allowance for a premium or a discount is made, due to the pro forma nature of the estimate.

Premiums and Discounts

Premiums and discounts are a very speculative area. According to H. Griffin Ewing Consultants, they are determined on the basis of:

1. projections due to lack of normal year performances, i.e., an increase of 82 percent in pretax income over the prior year;

2. a modest upswing percentage determination accorded to projected years.

Final Valuations

1.	Adjusted book value, December 31, 1975	$252,165
2.	Goodwill value	$606,895
3.	Valuation utilizing adjusted book method	$859,060
4.	Valuation utilizing adjusted capitalized earnings method	$732,975

CONCLUSIONS

Should an ESOP financial design be programmed for Profit Corp., Inc., a licensed Members Appraisal Institute (MAI) appraiser knowledgeable in valuing closely owned corporations should be engaged in order to determine "going in stock values" and to prepare for the Company a formula whereby future valuation can be ascertained.

Based on the above information, we believe that an Employee Stock Ownership Trust (ESOT) Plan could be structured somewhat along these lines:

1. The Company would adopt an ESOT Plan covering all full-time employees, with provisions for allocating Company contributions to employees of the Company in proportion to their relative compensation. The ESOP would be designed to qualify under Section 401(a) of the Internal Revenue Code as a tax-deductible Deferred Compensation Plan. The ESOT would be designed to invest in shares of common stock of the Company.

2. The contributions for fiscal year 1976 and all future contributions would be made to a combination Money Purchase Pension Plan and the ESOT. Pursuant to the Internal Revenue Code, these Company contributions would be tax deductible for state and federal income tax purposes, provided that such contributions do not exceed 25 percent of covered compensation (as defined in the Plan) paid to all eligible employees during each year.

3. The majority of stock now issued and to be issued would be planned as "outside stock," whereas A. B. Smith would always be in control of the Corporation. A block of stock, i.e., the remainder to be known as "inside stock," would be designated as ESOT Plan stock. Consequently, the Company would provide a means by which its employees, including the managerial executives, could acquire minority stock holdings with tax-deductible dollars rather than with aftertax dollars.

The following exhibits are included in this management analysis in order to show how an employee stock ownership trust, properly designed, will be of benefit to the Company, the employees, and the owner. For simplicity and exhibit reasoning, we have utilized the Company's current nine months' in-house profit-and-loss statements—combined with 1976–77 worksheet projections. We have figured financial results with and without ESOT and assumed percentage factors for the covered payroll and the pretax earnings of the Company.

Figures 6.1 through 6.4 show actual and projected gross sales and net earnings; they form exhibit 1 (pages 84–87). Exhibit 2 (below) provides some general information about ESOTs. Exhibit 3 (page 88) describes some recent ESOP implementations in Oregon. Exhibit 4 (page 89) gives five-year projections for U.S.A. Profit Co., Inc., with and without ESOT. These projections form tables 6.3–6.5.

Exhibit 2—General Information Regarding ESOTs

Often the management analysis refers to the word *ESOT*. This is an acronym for Employee Stock Ownership Trust. Originally, this word was limited to describing a qualified stock-bonus plan that purchased a substantial block of stock in the employer company in one single purchase with funds borrowed from a lender. The payments to the lender would be guaranteed by the employer corporation (U.S.A. Profit Co.), which could, if required by the lender, give a first lien on corporate properties such as inventory, machinery, equipment, and real estate. The advantage of one large purchase of stock, whether from a shareholder or from the corporation, is to leverage pretax benefits available to the plan where the equity value is growing faster than the interest being paid.

The word *ESOP*, Employee Stock Ownership Plan, is often used in an attempt to distinguish such plans from those using the original approach—i.e., one purchase of stock in a debt-retiring program. The ESOP (commonly referred to as a Stock Bonus Plan), as opposed to the ESOT, is used to acquire stock by purchases from stockholders or from the corporation only as contributions are received by the trust from the Company. In some circumstances, the contributions are paid to the trust by the Company in company stock, and no dollars ever change hands.

With the heightened interest in the stock bonus plan philosophy, the words *ESOT* and *ESOP* have become interchangeable by various writers and publications, and, for all practical purposes, the acronym *ESOT* has come to mean any type of stock bonus plan that is a qualified plan under Internal Revenue Code Section 401(a), the Tax Reduction Act (*P.L. 94-12*), and the Employee

FIG. 6.1.   ACTUAL GROSS SALES

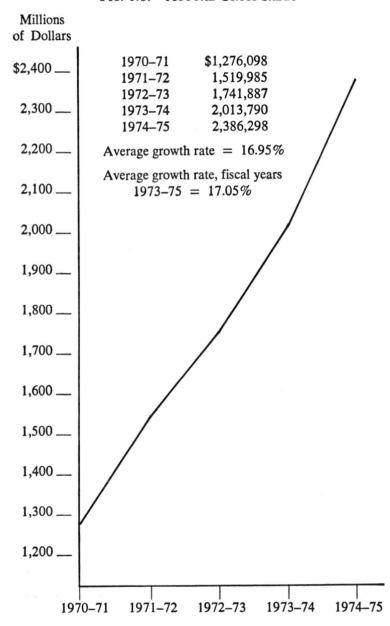

Millions
of Dollars

1970–71	$1,276,098
1971–72	1,519,985
1972–73	1,741,887
1973–74	2,013,790
1974–75	2,386,298

Average growth rate = 16.95%

Average growth rate, fiscal years
1973–75 = 17.05%

FIG. 6.2. ACTUAL NET EARNINGS

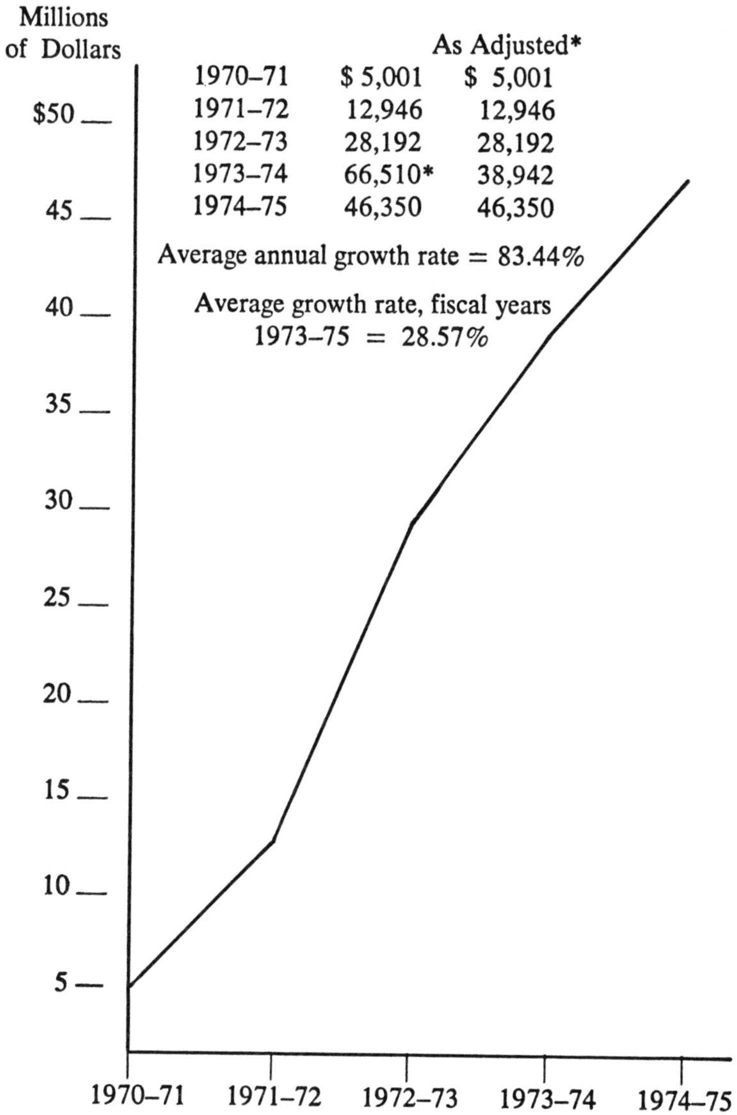

Millions
of Dollars

			As Adjusted*
	1970–71	$ 5,001	$ 5,001
	1971–72	12,946	12,946
	1972–73	28,192	28,192
	1973–74	66,510*	38,942
	1974–75	46,350	46,350

Average annual growth rate = 83.44%

Average growth rate, fiscal years
1973–75 = 28.57%

$50 —
45 —
40 —
35 —
30 —
25 —
20 —
15 —
10 —
5 —

1970–71   1971–72   1972–73   1973–74   1974–75

*Gain from sale of Company assets removed to reflect normal operations
($45,428 sale of asset in F.Y. 1973–74)

FIG. 6.3.   PROJECTED GROSS SALES
(based on 1976–77 in-house sales, 12-month analysis;
percentage factor at upswing average)

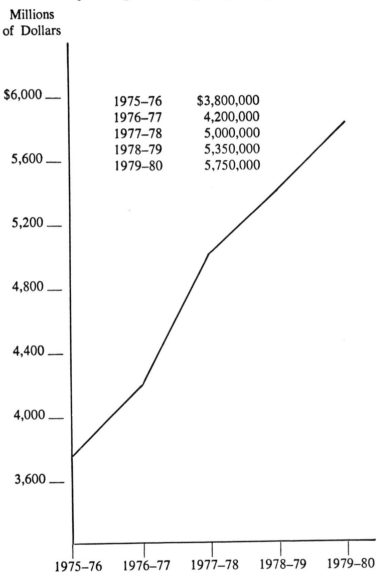

Millions
of Dollars

1975–76	$3,800,000
1976–77	4,200,000
1977–78	5,000,000
1978–79	5,350,000
1979–80	5,750,000

FIG. 6.4. PROJECTED NET INCOME

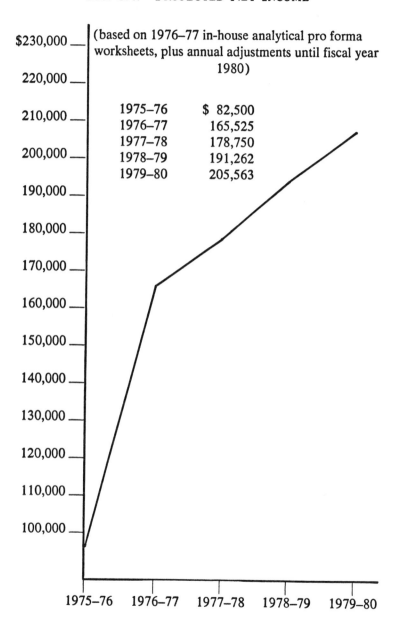

(based on 1976–77 in-house analytical pro forma worksheets, plus annual adjustments until fiscal year 1980)

1975–76	$ 82,500
1976–77	165,525
1977–78	178,750
1978–79	191,262
1979–80	205,563

Retirement Income Security Act of 1974. This book however voids interchangeableness primarily due to the author's understanding the purpose of the ESOT (trust) as a financial device that, to be meaningful, requires specification.

Following are three case histories of plans recently organized and completed in Oregon.

Exhibit 3—Recent ESOP Implementations in Oregon

Case 1 Albany International Industries (Rene Fritz, Jr., president), Albany manufacturer of sawmill equipment, organized in mid-1974 what is believed to be the first ESOP in Oregon. The purposes were to give employees the motivation of ownership and to convert pretax dollars into equity capital. The company has sales of $4 million a year and earlier had planned to go public. Albany puts 15 percent of payroll into ESOT (their qualified tax exempt trust) and, as in all such trusts, holds the pro rata amount in the name of each individual. In turn, the committee representing the trust uses these pretax dollars to buy the company's treasury stock.

Case 2 ESOT Printers, Inc. (Donald Bumgarner, president), Eugene printers, has twenty-six employees and installed an ESOT to finance a spin-off from a parent company, Graphic Arts, Inc., of Portland, Oregon. In November 1975, ESOT Printers, Inc., entered into a SBA-participating bank loan that enabled three executives of the company to acquire the business via a 90-10 loan to finance a deductible buy-out of capital stock. H. Griffin Ewing Consultants designed, organized, and implemented the plan.

Case 3 Gardner & Beedon (Al Turk, president), Portland wholesaler of plumbing and electrical supplies, gave its ESOT the added leverage of borrowing so that it could buy out the two founders who had started in 1947 with $3,000 and were ready to retire. This plan became final in the latter part of 1975, and the First National Bank of Oregon trust department was engaged to service it. The company converted its profit-sharing plan into an ESOT, which then used $300,000 of its own funds to buy the stock of the founders and borrowed enough from First National Bank of Oregon to complete the purchase. The ESOT will pay off the bank from Gardner & Beedon's annual payments of plan contributions.

Exhibit 4—Five-Year Projections for U.S.A. Profit Co.

TABLE 6.3. PRETAX INCOME, COVERED PAYROLL,
COMPANY CONTRIBUTIONS TO ESOT

Fiscal Year Ending March 31	Pretax Income	ESOT Participants' Payroll	Corporate Contribution to ESOT*	Percentage Factor
1976	$ 150,000	$ 435,000	$108,750	25
1977	300,956	465,000	116,250	25
1978	325,000	500,000	125,000	25
1979	347,750	540,000	135,000	25
1980	373,750	580,000	145,000	25
	$1,497,456	$2,520,000	$630,000	

*Contributions to ESOT should be made with a combination factor, i.e., cash less stock, and cash. This combination would permit cash to purchase retiring participants' stocks to provide funds for administration purposes—e.g., accounting, insurance investments, etc.—and to service the cost of long-term debt.

RECOMMENDATIONS

U.S.A. Profit Company's improvements, equipment, Company loans, note-due profit-sharing plan, and contracts, as of December 31, 1975, total $243,589 in long-term liabilities.

Conventional financing as per your financial statement of December 31, 1975, will require you to earn pretax income of $442,900 to repay $243,589 in principal amount of debt, assuming a federal effective income tax rate of 45 percent. Illustration:

$442,900	Pretax income
(199,311)	Less federal & state tax due
$243,589	Principal amount of long-term liabilities

1. Your cash-flow concernment requires that you take a strong look at pretax deductibles that will increase aftertax cash flow. Also, we recommend your comparing an ESOT financial design—with which you can now leverage a full 11 percent investment credit—with your present plans regard-

TABLE 6.4. CASH FLOW WITHOUT ESOT
(Assumption: continued cash bonus program)

Fiscal Year Ending March 31	1976	1977	1978	1979	1980
Pretax Earnings	$150,000	$300,956	$325,000	$347,750	$373,750
Fed. and State Corp. Income Tax	(67,500)	(135,431)	(146,250)	(156,488)	(168,187)
	$ 82,500	$165,525	$178,750	$191,262	$205,563

TABLE 6.5. CASH FLOW WITH ESOT

(Loan involved to retire present long-term debt and for financing new furniture store outlets. Pretax profits adjusted with regard to cash bonus projections.)

Fiscal Year Ending March 31	1976	1977	1978	1979	1980
Pretax Earnings	$150,000	$300,956	$325,000	$347,750	$373,750
Projected Bonus Adj.	45,000	44,000	54,000	55,250	59,500
Subtotal	$195,000	$344,956	$379,000	$403,000	$433,250
Minus deducts to ESOT:					
1. Stock	(67,750)	(41,375)	(49,375)	(63,625)	(102,875)
2. Cash for debt	(33,500)	(64,875)	(60,625)	(56,375)	(27,125)
3. Cash for liquidity	(7,500)	(10,000)	(15,000)	(15,000)	(15,000)
	$108,750	$116,250	$125,000	$135,000	$145,000
Taxable Income	$ 86,250	$228,706	$254,000	$268,000	$288,250
Income Tax	$ 38,813	$102,918	$114,300	$120,600	$129,713
Cash Flow	$115,187	$167,163	$189,075	$211,025	$261,412

ing purchase and/or leasing of equipment. The investment credit, being a direct offset against corporate tax, has maximum dollar usage, whereas a pretax dollar deduction is a divisional benefit to the Company.

2. Recapitulation of corporation taxes:

    Without an ESOT (table 6.4) $673,856
    With an ESOT retiring a
       $200,000 "new money loan" (table 6.5)   506,344

    Five-year reduction in corporation taxes $167,512

Special Note: Properly designed, the ESOT will permit both interest and principal to be amortized. Also note that cash flow can be substantially improved by donating authorized but unissued stock to the ESOT. (As per your December 31, 1975, financial statement prepared by the firm's C.P.A., your present unissued authorized stock account has 200 shares.)

3. If depreciation property is to be purchased, and the corporation acquires it with the proceeds of its sale of stock to the ESOT, the corporation will recover, over the life of the assets, more than 100 percent of the cost of new capital investment out of taxes, at current United States corporate income tax rates.

4. By financing through the stock-ownership trust, the Company's cash flow and net worth would increase substantially. If U.S.A. Profit Co., Inc., adopts an employee stock ownership trust, and the trust obtains a $200,000 bank loan guaranteed by the Company, U.S.A. Profit Co. can leverage pretax dollars rather than aftertax dollars. The trust purchases $200,000 worth of authorized stock, and the Company uses the $200,000 to finance new furniture store outlets. Thereafter, the Company makes annual tax-deductible contributions to the trust, which will be used to amortize the bank loan. By financing through the trust, the Company's cash flow and net worth will increase $200,000, and the Company will save corporation taxes. In addition, the loan does not appear as a liability on U.S.A. Profit Co., Inc., balance sheet, and the employees would be given a chance to share in the capital growth of the Company. The

FIG. 6.5.   SECOND INCOME PLAN TRUST
U.S.A. PROFIT CO., INC.

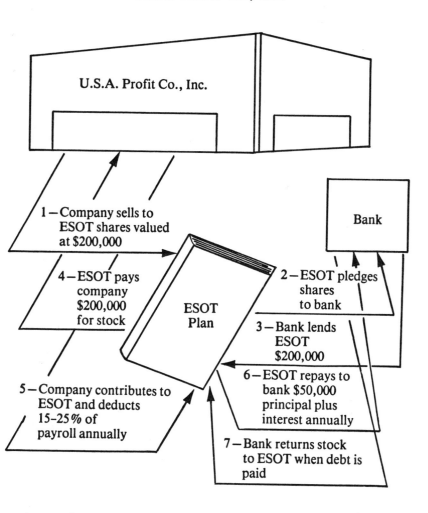

Assumptions:

$500,000 covered payroll
Loan factor $200,000 at 8½ percent interest
Annual payments $50,000
Refer to table 6.6 for trust cash flow
Refer to table 6.7 for debt amortization

ESOT plan will enable your bank loan officer to stretch the Company's cash flow; in turn, this enables you to service greater debt load. Servicing debt with pretax dollars means that debt can be amortized over a shorter period. The Second Income Plan (SIP) achieved through an ESOT is most potent, both in providing a source of financing for the Company and in enabling the employees to acquire equity ownership out of future savings. All present long-term debt is being paid with aftertax dollars.

Figure 6.5 is an illustration of how a Second Income Plan trust can enable U.S.A. Profit Co. to repay loan principal and interest with pretax dollars. This method of repayment can also be programmed to handle current company notes and contract obligations. Tables 6.6 and 6.7 are adjuncts to figure 6.5.

TABLE 6.6.   CASH FLOW SCHEDULE
OF THE TRUST (00's OMITTED)

RECEIPTS BY TRUST	1976	1977	1978	1979	1980
Present cash balance	$ 0	$ 7,5	$17,5	$32,5	$47,5
Contributions by Co.	41,0	74,9	75,6	71,4	42,1
Loan to Trust*	200,0	0	0	0	0
Cash Available	$241,0	$82,4	$93,1	$103,9	$89,6
DISBURSEMENTS BY TRUST					
Purchase of stock	$200,0	$ 0	$ 0	$ 0	$ 0
Payment of debt†	33,5	64,9	60,6	56,4	27,1
Repurchase of ESOT stock‡	0	0	0	0	0
Total Disbursements	$233,5	$64,9	$60,6	$56,4	$27,1
Ending Cash Balance	$ 7,5	$17,5	$32,5	$47,5	$62,5

*For this illustration, the stock and cash contribution annually has been programmed to reflect debt amortization of the loan, i.e., the same factors as table V.

†Amortization of bank loan at 4-year schedule, 1976 through 1980 (refer to table VII showing payment analysis).

‡Repurchasing participants' stock not analyzed for this illustration.

Summary: U.S.A. Profit Co., Inc., pays loan principal and interest with pretax dollars. Net aftertax cost to repay each dollar of principal and interest is 55 percent. (Illustration is computed at 45 percent effective federal taxes.) Cost to pay $200,000 is $110,000 plus aftertax cost of interest. Without an ESOT, U.S.A. Profit Co., Inc., would have to earn $363,700 to repay $200,000 principal.

TABLE 6.7. $200,000 AT 8½ PERCENT INTEREST
(Annual payments $50,000; 4-year amortization)

Fiscal Year Ending	Amount	Payments	Interest	Principal	Running Balance
1976 (6 mo.)	$200,000	$33,500	$8,500	$25,000	$175,000
1977 (year)	175,000	64,875	14,875	50,000	125,000
1978 (year)	125,000	60,625	10,625	50,000	75,000
1979 (year)	75,000	56,375	6,375	50,000	25,000
1980 (6 mo.)	25,000	27,125	2,125	25,000	0
		$242,500	$42,500	$200,000	

7

PLAN AND TRUST
AGREEMENT —
IRS APPROVED AND
QUALIFIED

Organizing and implementing a qualified plan and trust requires the practitioner to consider two major points: (1) tax advantages to the company, i.e., cash-flow gains created by the tax deduction; and (2) the long- and short-term needs of the client's business. Designing a plan to take advantage of both Section 401 of the IRS Code and recent legislation permitting the company to obtain 11 percent investment credit (Ref.: Section 301, Tax Reduction Act) enables the corporation to maximize both its own and the employees' financial position.

The following Plan and Trust Agreement illustrates one form of ESOP financial document. The unique design, titled a *94-6 percent deductible buy-out* by the author, was actually approved by the Seattle Office of Internal Revenue Employee Benefit Plans Division, and it was implemented by an Oregon firm in November 1976. (The name of the firm has been changed to ESOT Average, Inc.)

A total of 6 percent outside stock was structured to the three officers who were the management factor (three 2 percent executive shareholders), with the remaining 94 percent leveraged via bank and SBA participation in the financial plan.

ESOT AVERAGE, INC.,
EMPLOYEES' STOCK OWNERSHIP PLAN AND
TRUST AGREEMENT

Table of Contents

Article XIII.   *Miscellaneous*

13.1   Section Headings
13.2   Nonguarantee of Employment
13.3   Action by Employer
13.4   Nonalienation of Benefits
13.5   Applicable Law: Invalidity of Provisions
13.6   Fiduciary Liability Insurance
13.7   Participant's Benefits Limited to Trust Assets

Plan Provisions

ARTICLE I. NATURE OF PLAN

1.1 *Purpose.* The purpose of this Plan is to enable participating employees of the Company to share in the growth and prosperity of the Company and to provide participants with an opportunity to accumulate capital for their future economic security. The Plan is designed to do this without any deductions from participants' wages or without requiring the employees to invest their savings. A primary purpose of the Plan is to enable participants to acquire a proprietary interest in the Company. Consequently, the Employer contributions made to the Trust will be invested primarily in Company stock.

1.2 *Qualification.* This Plan, effective as of October 1, 1975, is intended to qualify as an Employee Stock Ownership Plan as defined in Section 4975 (e)(7) of the Internal Revenue Code and is a combination stock-bonus and money purchase plan, both of which are intended to qualify under Section 401(a) of the Internal Revenue Code. The Plan shall be administered by the Committee for the exclusive benefit of Participants and their Beneficiaries.

ARTICLE II. DEFINITIONS

In this Plan, whenever the context so indicates, the singular or plural number and the masculine, feminine, or neuter gender shall each be deemed to include the other; the terms *he, his,* and *him* shall refer to a participant of either gender; and the following words shall have the following meanings:

2.1 *Account* shall mean one of several accounts established and maintained to record the interest of a Participant in the Plan.

2.2 *Anniversary Date* shall mean the thirtieth day of September of each year.

2.3 *Authorized Leave of Absence* shall mean any absence of less than one year authorized by the Employer, provided that all persons under similar circumstances must be treated alike in the granting of such Authorized Leaves of Absence and provided further that written notice of such leave of absence is given to the Trustee by Employer at the commencement thereof, and the Employee returns to service with Employer on or before termination of the leave of absence. An absence due to active duty service in the armed forces of the United States, which may exceed one year, shall be considered an Authorized Leave of Absence provided that the absence is caused by war or other national emergency, and provided further that the Employee returns to service with the Employer within sixty days of termination of such service in the armed forces, or such longer period during which his employment rights may be protected by law.

2.4 *Beneficiary* shall mean the person or persons (natural or otherwise) designated by a Participant to receive any amounts payable under this Plan following the death of the Participant. The phrase *Participant or his Beneficiary* shall not confer any rights other than to the Participant during his lifetime.

2.5 *Board* shall mean the board of directors of Employer.

2.6 *Break in Service* shall mean a Plan Year in which a Participants fails to complete at least one Hour of Service (other than a failure which occurs in a Plan Year in which he retires, dies or suffers Disability).

2.7 *Committee* shall mean those persons selected under Section 9.1 to administer the Plan and to give instructions to the Trustee.

2.8 *Company* shall mean ESOT Average, Inc., an Oregon corporation.

2.9 *Company Stock* shall mean shares of any class of stock, preferred or common, voting or nonvoting, that is issued by the Company.

2.10 *Company Stock Account* shall mean the account of a Participant that is credited with the shares of Company Stock purchased and paid for by the Trust or contributed to the Trust.

2.11 *Covered Compensation* shall mean all amounts paid to a

Participant (gross compensation payable) by the Company for each year before deductions required by law or agreement, including overtime compensation, commissions, and bonuses, but excluding deferred compensation and contributions to this or any deferred compensation plan. Earnings shall be allocated to calendar years in the same manner as for federal income tax purposes.

2.12 *Current Obligations* shall mean Trust obligations arising from extension of credit to the Trust and payable in cash within one year from the date an Employer contribution is due.

2.13 *Disability* shall mean incapacity, resulting from bodily injury or disease, to engage in any occupation or employment for profit, unless resulting from drunkenness or addiction to narcotics, provided, however, that his incapacity has existed continuously for a period of at least six (6) months and provided further that it appears such incapacity shall continue during the remainder of such Participant's life. Any determination of Disability shall be made by the Committee, and its decision shall be final and conclusive with respect to any participant or other beneficiary hereunder.

2.14 *Effective Date* shall mean October 1, 1975, the date on which the provisions of this Plan became effective.

2.15 *Employee* shall mean any person who is employed by Employer and receiving remuneration.

2.16 *Employer* shall mean ESOT Average, Inc., and any successor business organization that elects to assume the obligations of this Plan.

2.17 *ERISA* shall mean the Employee Retirement Income Security Act of 1974, Public Law No. 93-406, as amended from time to time.

2.18 *Fiscal Year* shall mean the annual accounting period of the Employer.

2.19 *Forfeiture* shall mean the portion of a Participant's Accounts that does not become part of his Plan benefit.

2.20 *Fund* shall mean all of the assets held under the Plan by the Trustee.

2.21 *Hour of Service* shall mean each hour for which an Employee is either directly or indirectly compensated by the Employer or is performing duties for the Employer. *Hour of Service* shall also mean each hour for which back pay, irrespective of mitigation of damages, has been either awarded or agreed to by the Employer. Employees who are paid on a salaried, commission, or piecework basis, and whose compensation is not determined on the basis of certain amounts for each hour worked during a given period, shall be credited for forty (40) Hours of Service per week or pro rata portion thereof. The provisions of this definition of an Hour of Service shall be construed so that any ambiguities shall be resolved in favor of crediting Employees with Hours of Service.

2.22 *Named Fiduciary* shall mean the Employer, the Committee, and the Trustee, but only with respect to the specific responsibilities of each for Plan and Trust administration, all as described in Section 8.3 of this Plan.

2.23 *Normal Retirement Date* shall mean the date on which the Participant attains the age of sixty-five.

2.24 *Other Investments Account* shall mean the Account of the Participant is credited with his share of the net income (or loss) of the Trust and the Employer Contributions in other than Company Stock and that is debited with payments made to purchase Company Stock.

2.25 *Participant* shall mean any Employee who is eligible to participate in this Plan by meeting the requirements of Section 3.1.

2.26 *Plan* shall mean the ESOT Average, Inc., Employees' Stock Ownership Plan and Trust Agreement that is set forth herein and as it may be amended from time to time.

2.27 *Plan Administrator* shall mean the Committee.

2.28 *Plan Year* shall mean the twelve-month period ending on each Anniversary Date.

2.29 *Semiannual Entry Date* shall mean an April 1 or October 1 occurring after October 1, 1975.

2.30 *Service* shall mean a Participant's period of employment with the Employer determined in accordance with Section 3.2.

2.31 *Trust* shall mean the trust created by the Trust Agreement between the Employer and the Trustee entered into herein.

2.32 *Trustee* shall mean the person or persons appointed by the Board to administer the Trust.

ARTICLE III. ELIGIBILITY AND PARTICIPATION

3.1 *Eligibility Requirements.* Every Employee will become a Participant in this Plan on the first day of the Plan Year following his attainment of age twenty-five and his first Hour of Service.

3.2 *Participation.* As of each Anniversary Date, a Participant is entitled to the allocations provided in Article V. An Employee who becomes a Participant shall be credited with a Year of Service for each of the following periods during which he completes 1,000 or more Hours of Service:

(a) The twelve-month period following the day on which the Employee performs his first Hour of Service, and

(b) The Plan Year which includes the last day of the period described in subparagraph (a) of this Section 3.2 and each successive Plan Year.

3.3 *Leave of Absence.* Employment shall not be deemed to have been interrupted for purposes of Participation and Break in Service under this Plan by reason of Authorized Leaves of Absence. The Participant shall not be entitled to share in the Employer contributions to the Plan during his absence except to the extent entitled by virtue of Compensation received by him in the year in which he leaves. He shall continue to share in gains and losses during his authorized absence in accordance with Section 5.3 (c).

An Employee who fails to return to active employment at or before the expiration of this Authorized Leave of Absence, shall be deemed to have separated from service as of the time a separation from service would have occurred but for this Section 3.3; however, he shall forfeit any amounts credited to his Account during his absence, along with any increases in his vested amount at the earliest time that it can be determined that the employee has had a Break in Service. However, if such Participant's failure to return to work results from death or Disability, his Participation shall be deemed to have continued until the date of his death or of the termination of his employment for Disability. In exercising any discretion under this Section 3.3, the Employer shall treat all Employees similarly situated in a nondiscriminatory manner.

3.4 *Inactive Status.* In the event that any Participant shall fail, in any Plan Year of his employment after the Effective Date, to accumulate 1,000 Hours of Service, his Account shall be placed on Inactive Status. In such case, such year shall not be considered as a period of Service for the purposes of determining the Participant's vested interest in accordance with Section 7.4, and the Participant shall not share in the contribution made by Employer, but he shall continue to share in the net income (or loss) of the Trust in accordance with Section 5.3(c).

3.5 *Participation and Service upon Reemployment.* Participation in the Plan shall cease whenever a Participant incurs a Break in Service. Such Break in Service may have resulted from retirement, voluntary or involuntary termination of employment, unauthorized absence, or by failure to return to active employment with the Employer by the date on which an Authorized Leave of Absence expired.

Upon the reemployment of any person after the Effective Date who has incurred a Break in Service on or after the Effective Date, the following rules shall apply in determining his Participation in the Plan and his Years of Service under Section 3.2:

(a) Participation. The reemployed Employee will become a Participant beginning with the first Hour of Service on his reemployment date.

(b) Service. Any service attributable to his prior period of employment shall be reinstated as of the date of his Participation.

ARTICLE IV. CONTRIBUTIONS

4.1 *Employer Contributions.* For each Plan Year, the Employer will contribute to the Trust an amount as follows:

(a) For the money purchase plan, 10 percent of all Participants' Covered Compensation (exclusive of inactive Participants' Compensation), and

(b) For the stock bonus plan, such amount (not to exceed 15 percent of all Participants' Covered Compensation exclusive of inactive Participants' Compensation) as may be determined by Board resolution adopted on or before the last day of the Plan Year. In the absence of such a resolution, the amount to be contributed shall be 15 percent of Covered Compensation. However, the Employer Contributions for each year shall never be less than the amount required to enable the Trust to discharge its current obligations.

In no event, however, shall such Employer Contribution for the fiscal year exceed 25 percent of the aggregate Compensation

otherwise paid or accrued by the Employer to the Participants for
the fiscal year, increased by such amounts as may be carried forward under the provisions of Section 404(a)(3)(A) of the Internal Revenue Code of 1954, or any amendments thereto, as in
existence at the date of the contribution, but not to exceed the
maximum deductible amount.

All amounts contributed by the Employer to this Plan shall
be made for the exclusive benefit of the Participants and their
Beneficiaries and in no event shall any contribution by the Employer or income therefrom revert to the Employer except as provided in Section 8.2.

The amount of the Employer Contribution for each year will
be communicated to the Participants on or prior to each Anniversary Date.

4.2 *Voluntary Participant Contributions.* No Participant shall
be required or permitted to make contributions to the Trust.

4.3 *Form of Contributions.* Employer Contributions will be paid
in cash, shares of Company Stock, or in other property as the
Board may from time to time determine. Shares of Company
Stock and other property will be valued at the fair market value
at the time of the contribution. However, to the extent that the
Trust has current obligations, the Employer Contributions will be
paid to the Trust in cash.

4.4 *Time of Contributions.* The obligation to pay the contribution above provided shall accrue as of the last day of any Plan
Year and shall be paid to the Trustee as soon as convenient after
the close of any Plan Year, but in any event within the time prescribed by law for filing the Employer's federal income tax return,
including extensions.

ARTICLE V. ALLOCATION OF ACCOUNTS

There shall be separate accounting for the Employer Contributions made pursuant to Sections 4.1(a) and 4.1(b). The
following Sections of this Article V describe the types of Participant Accounts that will be established, the kinds of Allocations
that will be made, and the Maximum Annual Additions that can
be made to the Participants' Accounts.

5.1 *Company Stock Account.* The Company Stock Account of

each Participant will be credited as of each Anniversary Date with his allocable share of Company Stock (including fractional shares) purchased and paid for by the Trust or contributed in kind by the Employer, with stock dividends on Company Stock held in his Company Stock Account. Where shares of Company Stock have been purchased by the Trust under an installment payment contract or with borrowed funds, the allocation of shares of Company Stock to Participant's Company Stock Accounts will be "Contingent" to the extent that shares have been allocated subject to the rights of the seller or lender, as the case may be, to secure payment in full of the purchase price or the balance of any outstanding loan. Notwithstanding any other provision of the Plan, shares of Company Stock that are Contingent shall not be distributed to a Participant. The number of shares of Company Stock in a Participant's Company Stock Account that are Contingent shall be determined by multiplying the total number of shares of Company Stock in such Company Stock Account by the ratio of: (1) the total number of shares of Company Stock allocated to all Participants' Company Stock Accounts less the aggregate number of shares that are not subject to contingency restrictions hereunder, to (2) the total number of shares of Company Stock allocated to all Participants' Company Stock Accounts. The contingency restrictions referred to in this Section 5.1 and in Section 7.5 shall lapse at such time as the said ratio becomes 5 percent or less.

The share of a Participant whose employment was terminated for any reason after the end of the Plan Year, but prior to the date of receipt by the Trustee of the full or remaining contribution by the Employer for the Plan Year in question, shall be determined and distributed by the Trustee to such Participant or his Beneficiary in accordance with the pertinent provisions of this Plan as if such share had been available on his termination date.

5.2 *Other Investments Account.* The Other Investments Account of each Participant so entitled will be credited (or debited) as of each Anniversary Date with his share of the net income (or loss) of the Trust, with cash dividends on Company Stock in his Company Stock Account, and with Employer Contributions in other than Company Stock. It will be debited for any payments on purchases of Company Stock or for repayment of debt (including principal and interest) incurred for the purchase of Company Stock, and with his share of insurance premium payments, if any.

5.3 *Allocations.* The allocations will be made as follows:

(a) Employer Contributions. Employer Contributions will be allocated as of each Anniversary Date among the Accounts of Participants so entitled in the ratio in which the Covered Compensation of each bears to the aggregate Covered Compensation of all such Participants for that year.

(b) Forfeitures. In the event of termination of employment of a Participant for reasons other than retirement at the Normal Retirement Date, Disability, or death, the amount of such Participant's Accounts that is not fully vested shall be used to reduce the Employer's current and/or subsequent year's contributions under this Plan. However, Forfeitures will not be available to reduce Employer Contributions until the Participant who forfeited has incurred a Break in Service.

(c) Net Income (or Loss) of the Trust. The net income (or loss) of the Trust will be determined annually as of each Anniversary Date. A share thereof will be allocated to each Participant's Other Investments Account in the ratio in which the balance of his Other Investments Account on the preceding Anniversary Date bears to the sum of the balances for the Other Investment Accounts of all Participants on that date. The net income (or loss) includes the increase (or decrease) in the fair market value of assets of the Trust (other than Company Stock in the Company Stock Accounts), interest, dividends, other income, and expenses attributable to assets in the other investments accounts since the preceding Anniversary Date. It does not include the interest paid under any installment contract for the purchase of Company Stock by the Trust or on any loan used by the Trust to purchase Company Stock.

(d) Life Insurance Policies. In the event that the Committee directs the Trustee to invest in a life insurance policy on the life of any "key-man" employee, such policy shall be held as an investment for the benefit of the Trust. Death proceeds received on any life insurance policy, and insurance premiums with respect to such policy, shall be allocated among the Accounts of Participants in the same manner as provided in Section 5.3(c). Participants bear to the total of such debits for all Participants as of the next Anniversary Date.

5.4 *Separate Individual Accounts.* The Committee shall establish and maintain separate individual accounts for each Participant in the Plan. Separate accounts shall be maintained for all inactive Participants who have an interest in the Plan. Such separate accounts shall not require a segregation of the Trust assets, and no Participant shall acquire any right to or interest in any specific asset of the Trust as a result of the allocations provided for in the Plan. All allocations will be made as of the Anniversary Date referred to in this Article.

5.5 *Maximum Annual Additions.* Notwithstanding anything contained herein to the contrary, Annual Additions to all of Participant's Accounts for any Plan Year after 1975 shall not exceed the lesser of $25,000 or 25 percent of the Participant's Compensation for such year.

Annual Additions shall mean the total of Employer Contributions allocated to all of Participant's Accounts during the Plan Year.

Notwithstanding the foregoing, the otherwise permissible Annual Additions for any Participant under this Plan may be further reduced to the extent necessary, as determined by the Committee, to prevent disqualification of the Plan under Section 415 of the Internal Revenue Code, which imposes additional limitations on the benefits payable to Participants who also may be participating in another tax-qualified pension, profit-sharing, savings, or stock-bonus plan of the Employer. The Committee shall advise affected Participants of any additional limitation of their Annual Additions required by the preceding sentence.

ARTICLE VI. VALUATION AND ANNUAL STATEMENT

6.1 *Annual Valuation.* The Trustee, as of the close of business on the last day of each Plan Year, prior to the allocation of Employer Contributions as provided under Section 5.3(a), shall determine the net value of the Trust Fund assets and the amount of net income or net loss and shall report such value to the Employer in writing.

In determining such value, the Trustee shall value all assets at fair market value as of the close of business on the last day of each Plan Year. The determination of such value shall not include any contributions made by the Employer for such Plan Year or any policies. The resulting net income or loss of the Trust Fund shall then be debited or credited to each Participant's Account in the same ratio as each Account bears to the aggregate of all such Accounts. After such crediting of the valuation to each Account, contributions shall be allocated to each Account as set forth in Sections 5.3(a). This provision shall be administered in a uniform and nondiscriminatory manner.

6.2 *Annual Statement.* As soon as practicable after each Anniversary Date, the Employer shall present to each Participant a statement of his Account showing the credit to his Account at the beginning of such Year, any changes during the Year, the credit to his Account at the end of the Year, and such other information as the Employer may determine. However, neither the maintenance of Accounts, the allocation of credits to Accounts, nor the statements of Account shall operate to vest in any Participant any right or interest in or to any assets of the Trust except as the Plan specifically provides.

ARTICLE VII. DISTRIBUTION OF BENEFITS

7.1 *Retirement.* If a Participant's employment with the Employer is terminated at or after he attains the Normal Retirement Date, he shall be entitled to receive the entire amount then in his Accounts in accordance with Sections 7.5 and 7.6.

7.2 *Disability.* If a Participant's employment with the Employer is terminated at an age earlier than the Normal Retirement Date because of Disability, he shall be entitled to receive the entire amount then in his Accounts in accordance with Sections 7.5 and 7.6.

7.3 *Death.* In the event that the termination of employemnt of a Participant is caused by his death, the entire amount then in his Accounts shall be paid to his Beneficiary or Beneficiaries in accordance with Sections 7.5 and 7.6.

7.4 *Termination for Other Reasons.* If a Participant's employment with the Employer is terminated prior to his Normal Retirement Date for any reason other than Disability or death, the Participant shall be entitled to his Vested Percentage of his Accounts.

Such Vested Percentage shall be determined in accordance with the following schedule:

Years of Service	Vested Percentage
1	20%
2	40%
3	60%
4	80%
5	100%

Years of Service on the above schedule shall be determined in accordance with Section 3.2.

Payment of benefits due under this Section shall be made in accordance with Sections 7.5 and 7.6.

7.5 *Time of Distribution.* A Participant's Plan benefit will be computed and paid to him not later than sixty (60) days after the end of the Plan Year in which the Participant retires, dies, suffers Disability, or has a Break in Service. The Participant will be entitled to receive all or a portion of his Accounts pursuant to Sections 7.1 through 7.4. The Participant will have distributed to him the number of shares of Company Stock that have been allocated to his Accounts and that are unencumbered. Any shares of Contingent Stock that are subject to the contingency restrictions described in Section 5.1 shall not be distributed to the Participant.

The Committee, after considering the wishes of the Participant or his Beneficiary, will direct the Trustee to distribute the Participant's plan benefit consisting of unencumbered stock in accordance with one or more of the following ways or in a combination of them:

(a) In a lump sum or single payment;

(b) In substantially equal annual, quarterly, or monthly installments plus accrued net income (or loss). This may be based on a fixed number of years or a fixed percentage of his Plan benefit. However, the period of installments may not exceed his life expectancy, or the joint life expectancy of the Participant and his spouse. If the Participant or his Beneficiary should die prior to the expiration of the distribution period, the balance of the payments shall be made to his Beneficiary or Beneficiaries as provided in Section 7.9.

In any event, unless the Participant otherwise elects, the payment of benefits to the Participant will begin not later than the

(60th) day after the close of the Plan Year in which the latest of the following events occurs: (1) the Participant attains the Normal Retirement Date (age sixty-five); (2) the tenth anniversary of the year in which the Participant commenced participation in the Plan, or (3) the Participant terminates his Service with the Employer. However, a Participant must commence receiving benefits within five years of his actual retirement date.

7.6 *Form of Distribution.* Distribution of Plan benefits will be made entirely in whole shares of Company Stock. Any balance in a Participant's Other Investments Account will be applied to acquire for distribution the maximum number of whole shares of Company Stock at the then fair market value. Any amount remaining in the Participant's Other Investment Account that is insufficient to purchase a whole share of Company Stock shall be distributed in cash. The Trustee will make distribution from the Trust only on instructions from the Committee.

7.7 *Incompetency of Recipient.* If the Committee determines that a person entitled to any distribution is physically unable or mentally incompetent to receive such distribution, it may direct the Trustee to apply such distribution for such person's benefit.

7.8 *Late Retirement.* Every Participant shall retire upon reaching the Normal Retirement Date, except that the Participant and Employer may agree that Participant shall continue to be employed by Employer. In the event of such employment subsequent to the Normal Retirement Date, such Employee shall continue to participate in the Plan until death or termination of his employment. The payment of benefits shall be deferred until actual retirement at which time payment shall be made in accordance with Sections 7.5 and 7.6.

7.9 *Designation of Beneficiary.* Upon becoming a Participant, every Employee may designate a Beneficiary or Beneficiaries to receive his interest in the Fund upon his death, and thereafter at any time and without notice to any Beneficiary a Participant may change any such designation of Beneficiary previously made by him. A Designation of Beneficiary shall be made in accordance with the rules established by the Committee and upon such form as the Committee may designate. No designation of Beneficiary shall be valid or effective for any purpose or binding upon the Trustee until it has been received by the Trustee.

In the absence of a designation of Beneficiary by the Participant, payment in the event of death shall be made in the following order of priority: First to surviving spouse, second to children in equal shares with a share by right of representation to the then surviving children of any deceased child, third to parents in equal shares or to the surviving parent, fourth to heirs as determined by the intestacy laws of the state of Oregon.

Upon making payment in the event of death to the former Participant's designated Beneficiary or Beneficiaries, or to the Beneficiaries above named if the Participant has no valid Designation of Beneficiary in effect at the time of his death, the Trustee and the Fund shall be relieved of any further obligation and neither the Trustee nor the Fund shall be liable to any other person or claimant.

7.10 *Plan Benefits Awaiting Distribution.* Any part of a Participant's plan benefit which is retained in the Trust after the Anniversary Date on which his participation ends will continue to be treated as a Company Stock Account or as an Other Investments Account, as the case may be, as provided in Article V. However, neither Account will be credited with any further Employer contributions. His Accounts will, however, share in the net income (or loss) of the Trust as provided in Section 5.3(c) and allocations provided for in Section 5.3(d). The Trustee, upon direction of the Employer, may place such undistributed funds in a segregated account by deposit in a savings bank for the payment of interest thereon, or otherwise. Any such segregated account shall not be considered an Account for purposes of Article V and shall not share in net gains and losses as provided in Section 5.3(c).

7.11 *Loans to Participants.* The Trustee may, if the Committee consents, lend a Participant an amount not in excess of 50 percent of the vested portion of his Accounts as of the date on which the loan is approved. All loans shall be subject to the approval of the Committee, which shall thoroughly investigate each application for a loan. Loans shall be permitted for extraordinary or emergency expenditures only and shall not exceed the actual amount of such extraordinary or emergency needs. Loans made by the Plan shall be available to all Participants and Beneficiaries on a reasonably equivalent basis. Loans shall not be made available to highly compensated Employees, officers, or shareholders in an amount greater than the amount made available to other Employees.

In addition to such rules and regulations as the Committee may adopt, all loans shall comply with the following terms and conditions:

(a) An application for a loan by a Participant shall be made in writing to the Committee, whose action thereon shall be final.

(b) The period of repayment for any loan shall be arrived at by mutual agreement between the Committee and the borrower, but such period in no event shall exceed the lesser of ten (10) years or the remaining period of time to the Participant's Normal Retirement Date.

(c) The loan shall be adequately secured.

(d) Each loan shall bear interest at a rate to be fixed by the Committee and, in determining the interest rate, the Committee shall take into consideration interest rates currently being charged. The Committee shall not discriminate among Participants in the matter of interest rates; but loans granted at different times may bear different interest rates if, in the opinion of the Committee, the difference in rates is justified by a change in general economic conditions.

(e) No Plan benefit shall be reduced by any outstanding loan balance existing at the time a distribution is called for under this Plan.

7.12 *Rights and Options on Distributed Shares of Company Stock.* Shares of Company Stock distributed by the Trustee may, as determined by the Company or the Committee, be subject to a Right of First Refusal. Such a Right shall provide that, prior to any subsequent transfer, the shares must first be offered in writing to the Trust and then, if refused by the Trust, to the Company at the then fair market value or the price offered by a third party, whichever price is higher. The Trust or Company, as the case may be, may accept the offer at any time during a period not exceeding thirty (30) days after receipt of such offer. If the Trust or Company rejects the offer, evidence of such decision shall be stated in writing to the former Participant.

In the discretion of the Committee, exercised in a uniform, nondiscriminatory manner, a Participant may be granted at the time that shares of Company Stock are distributed to him, an option to "put" the shares, or any part of them, to the Trust and/or the Company. A "put" option shall provide that, for a period of up to sixty (60) days after such shares are distributed to a Participant or Beneficiary, he would have the right to have the Trust and/or the Company, as the "put" may specify, purchase such shares at their fair market value. The terms of payment for the purchase of such shares of stock shall be as set forth in the "put" and may be either in a lump sum or in substantially equal annual, quarterly, or monthly payments over a period not to exceed five (5) years from the date of exercise of the "put" option, with interest on the unpaid principal balance at the rate currently charged by commercial lending institutions in the community.

Trust and Administrative Provisions

ARTICLE VIII. ADMINISTRATION

8.1 *The Fund.* All assets deriving from the administration of the Plan, including all contributions, gains, earnings, and proceeds from insurance policies, shall be owned and held by the Trustee. Any such assets of the Fund may be registered, or title may be held in the name of ESOT Average, Inc., Employees' Trust. All assets of the Fund shall be retained for the exclusive benefit of Participants, former Participants, and Beneficiaries and shall be used to pay benefits to such persons or to pay administrative expenses of the Plan to the extent not paid by the Employer, and shall not revert to or inure to the benefit of the Employer.

8.2 *Return of Employer Contributions.* Notwithstanding anything herein to the contrary, upon the Employer's request, a contribution that was conditioned upon initial qualification of the Plan shall be returned to the Employer in the event the Plan does not initially qualify.

8.3 *Allocation of Responsibility among Named Fiduciaries.* The Named Fiduciaries shall have only those specific powers, duties, responsibilities, and obligations as are specifically given them under this Plan. In general, the Employer shall have the sole responsibility for making the contributions provided for under Article IV, and shall have the sole authority to appoint and remove the Trustee and Members of the Committee. The Employer shall also have sole authority to amend or terminate, in whole or in part, this Plan as well as the Trust created within this Plan. The Committee shall have the sole responsibility for the administration of this Plan, which responsibility is specifically described in Article IX. The Trustee shall have the sole responsibility for the administration of the Trust and the management of the assets held under the Trust. The Trustee's powers, duties, responsibilities, and obligations are specifically described in Article X of this Plan.

Each Named Fiduciary warrants that any directions given, information furnished, or action taken by it shall be in accordance with the provisions of the Plan, as the case may be, authorizing or providing for such direction, information, or action. Furthermore, each Named Fiduciary may rely upon any such direction, information, or action of another Named Fiduciary as being proper under this Plan, and is not required under this Plan to inquire into the propriety of any such direction, information, or action. It is intended under this Plan that each Named Fiduciary shall be responsible for the proper exercise of its own powers, duties, responsibilities, and obligations under this Plan and shall not be responsible for any act or failure to act of another Named Fiduciary. None of the Named Fiduciaries guarantees the Fund in any manner against investment loss or depreciation in asset value.

Any person may serve in more than one fiduciary capacity with respect to this Plan, specifically including service both as a Trustee and as Plan Administrator, subject to the separate requirements of Sections 9.1 and 10.1 that such acceptances be severally evidenced.

ARTICLE IX. ADMINISTRATIVE COMMITTEE

9.1 *Appointment of Committee.* The Plan shall be administered by the Committee consisting of at least three persons who shall be appointed by and serve at the pleasure of the Board. The Board shall have no responsibility for the operation and administration of the Plan. Those persons so designated as members of the Committee shall signify their acceptance of this responsibility by joining in the execution of the documents adopting this Plan. All usual and reasonable expenses of the Committee may be paid in whole or in part by the Employer, and any expenses not paid by the Employer shall be paid by the Trustee out of the principal and income of the Fund. Any members of the Administrative Committee who are Employees shall not receive compensation with respect to their services for the Committee. Vacancies in the Committee arising by reason of resignation, death, removal, or otherwise shall be filled by the Board. Any member of the Committee may resign of his own accord by delivering his written resignation to the Employer.

9.2 *Rights, Powers, and Duties of Committee.* The Committee shall have the following rights, powers, and duties in addition to those set forth elsewhere in the Plan or by law:

(a) The Committee shall give instructions to the Trustee as to how Company Stock held by the Trustee is to be voted.

(b) The Committee may employ investment managers and advisors, accountants, legal counsel, consultants, and such other persons as it shall deem necessary or desirable to assist it in the performance of its duties under the Plan.

(c) The Committee shall determine any questions arising in the administration, interpretation, and application of the Plan, which determination shall be binding and conclusive on all persons.

(d) The Committee is authorized to make and publish such rules and regulations as it may deem necessary to carry out the provisions of the Plan.

(e) The Committee shall compute, certify, and direct the Trustee with respect to the amount and kind of benefits to which any Participant or Beneficiary shall be entitled hereunder.

(f) The Committee shall establish and maintain Accounts and records to record the interest of each Participant, inactive Participant, and their respective Beneficiaries in the Plan.

(g) The Committee shall establish and maintain accounts showing the fiscal transactions of the Plan. The Committee shall prepare annually a report showing in reasonable detail the assets and liabilities of the Plan and giving a brief account of the operation of the Plan for the past year. In preparing this report the Committee may rely on advice received from the Trustee or other persons or firms selected by it or may adopt a report on such matters prepared by the Trustee. Such report shall be submitted to the Board and shall be filed in the office of the Secretary of the Committee.

(h) The Committee shall exercise such authority and responsibility as it deems appropriate in order to comply with ERISA and governmental regulations issued thereunder relating to records of Participant's Service, account balances, and the percentage of such account balances that are nonforfeitable under the Plan; notifications to Participants; annual registration with the Internal Revenue Service; and annual reports to the Department of Labor.

(i) The Committee shall authorize and direct the Trustee with respect to all disbursements from the Trust.

(j) The Committee may prescribe procedures to be followed by Participants or Beneficiaries filing applications for benefits.

(k) The Committee is authorized to prepare and distribute, in such manner as it determines to be appropriate, information explaining the Plan.

9.3 *Organization and Operation of Committee.* The Committee may act at a meeting or in writing without a meeting. The Committee shall elect one of its members as Chairman, appoint a Secretary, who may or may not be a Committee member, and advise the Trustee of all such actions in writing. The Secretary shall keep a record of all meetings and forward all necessary communications to the Employer or the Trustee. The Committee may adopt such bylaws and regulations as it deems desirable for the conduct of its affairs. All decisions of the Committee shall be made by the vote of the majority including actions in writing taken without a meeting. The Committee may by such majority action authorize any one or more members of the Committee to execute any document or documents on behalf of the Committee. A dissenting Committee member who, within a reasonable time after he has knowledge of any action or failure to act by the majority, registers his dissent in writing delivered to the other Committee members, the Employer and the Trustee, shall not be responsible for any such action or failure to act.

9.4 *Application for Benefits.* All applications for benefits under the Plan shall be submitted to the personnel department of the Employer. Applications for benefits must be in writing on the forms prescribed by the Committee and must be signed by the Participant and, if required by the Committee his spouse, or in the case of a death benefit, by the beneficiary or legal representative of the deceased Participant. The Committee reserves the right to require that the Participant furnish proof of his age prior to processing any application. Each application shall be acted upon and approved or disapproved within sixty (60) days following its receipt by the personnel department. In the event any application for benefits is denied, in whole or in part, the Employer shall notify the applicant in writing of such denial and of his right to a review by the Committee and shall set forth, in a manner calculated to be understood by the applicant, specific reasons for such denial, specific references to pertinent Plan provisions on which the denial is based, a description of any additional material or information necessary for the applicant to perfect his application, an explanation of why such material or information is necessary and an explanation of the Plan's review procedure and the method of appeal from the decision.

9.5 *Indemnity.* The Employer shall indemnify and hold harmless each member of the Committee from any and all claims, loss, damages, expense (including counsel fees approved by the Committee), and liability (including any amounts paid in settlement with the Committee's approval) arising from any act or omission of such member, except when the same is judicially determined to be due to the gross negligence or willful misconduct of such member.

ARTICLE X. TRUSTEE PROVISIONS

10.1 *Creation and Acceptance of Trust.* The Trustee, by joining in the execution of the documents adopting this Plan, accepts the Trust hereby created and agrees to act in accordance with the express terms and conditions stated herein.

10.2 *Trustee Capacity.* The Trustee may be a bank, trust company, or other corporation possessing trust powers under applicable state or federal law, or one or more individuals, or any combination thereof.

10.3 *Resignation and Removal of Trustee.* The Board shall have the power to remove a Trustee by delivering to such Trustee a certified copy of a resolution of the Board to that effect. A Trustee may resign as Trustee upon giving written notice to the Employer. Such removal or resignation shall become effective on the date specified in such resolution or such written notice, which date shall not be less than thirty (30) days subsequent to the delivery of such resolution or written notice. In the event of such removal or resignation, a successor Trustee shall be appointed by the Board.

Upon receipt by the Trustee of written acceptance of such appointment of a successor Trustee, the Trustee shall convey, assign, and deliver to such successor Trustee the assets of the Trust, together with all records pertaining thereto. The Trustee is authorized, however, to reserve such assets as it may deem advisable for payment of all fees, compensations, costs, and expenses, or for payment of any other liabilities constituting a charge on or against the assets of the Trust or on or against the Trustee, with any balance remaining after the payment of all such items to be paid over to the successor Trustee. The successor Trustee shall have all right, title, and interest in the assets paid over to it, and all power, rights, and duties under the Trust vested in the Trustee shall vest in such successor Trustee immediately upon its appointment and acceptance, and thereupon all further duties and liabilities of the Trustee that have been succeeded shall terminate except for an accounting as may be required.

10.4 *Fees, Taxes, Expenses, and Collection.*

(a) Fees. The Trustee in consideration of its services under the Trust shall receive such fee as the Employer agrees to pay to the Trustee. The Trustee may change such fees at any time upon thirty (30) days' written notice to the Employer, or may agree to waive fees.

(b) Taxes. Any income, gift, estate, and inheritance taxes and other taxes of any kind whatsoever, including transfer taxes incurred in connection with the investment, reinvestment, or distribution of the assets of the Trust, that may be levied or assessed in respect to such assets or the income thereon shall, if allocable to the Account or interest of specific Participants, be charged to such Accounts or interests, and if not so allocable they shall be charged proportionately to the Accounts or interests of all Participants, or to the Employer, as the circumstances shall require.

(c) Expenses. All other administrative expenses incurred by the Trustee in the performance of its duties, including fees for legal services rendered to the Trustee, shall be paid by the Employer within thirty (30) days after a statement of such expenses is rendered by the Trustee to the Employer.

(d) Collection. All fees of the Trustee and taxes and other administrative expenses charged to the Trust shall, at the Trustee's option, be paid by the Employer to the Trustee with the amount of the first contribution for each Trust Year that is to be credited to the Trust, or by sale or liquidation of the assets credited to the Trust if no contribution is made thereto in that Year; and if the assets of the Trust are insufficient to satisfy such charges, the Employer shall pay any deficit therein to the Trustee.

10.5 *Rights, Powers, and Duties of Trustee.* The Trustee shall have the following rights, powers, and duties in addition to those set forth elsewhere in the Plan or by law:

(a) Receipt of Contributions. The Trustee shall not be responsible in any way for the collection of contributions provided for under the Trust. The Trustee shall accept and hold under the Trust such contributions of money, or other property approved by the Employer for acceptance by the Trustee, on behalf of the Employer and Participants as it may receive from time to time from the Employer. All such contributions shall be accompanied by written instructions from the Employer accounting for the manner in which they are to be credited.

(b) Settlement of Claims. The Trustee shall have the power and duty to settle, compromise, or submit to arbitration any claims, debts, or damages due or owing to or from the Trust; and to commence or defend any legal or administrative proceedings brought in connection with this Plan whenever, in its judgment, any interest of the Trust requires it.

(c) Borrowing. The Trustee may borrow, from banks or similar lending institutions, reasonable sums of money for the purchase of Company Stock for the Accounts of Participants. The Trustee may not borrow from itself or an affiliated institution, even if it is a bank or similar lending institution.

(d) Distributions. On receipt of a written order from the Committee certifying that a Participant's benefits are payable pursuant to the Trust, the Trustee shall take such action as may be necessary to make distribution in such form and at such time as the order of payment so directs. However, before making any such distribution in the event of a Participant's death, the Trustee shall be furnished with any and all certificates, tax waivers, and other documents that may be requested in its discretion.

(e) Retention of Cash Balances. The Trustee may temporarily retain a portion of the funds of the Trust in cash or cash balances and shall be entitled to deposit such funds in a bank account or bank accounts in the name of ESOT Average, Inc., Employees' Trust in any bank or banks selected by Trustee, including the Banking Department of the Trustee. Any such deposit may be made with or without interest.

(f) Records of Administration. The Trustee shall keep accurate and detailed records of its administration of this Plan and Trust, which records shall be open to inspection at all reasonable times by the Committee. A Participant shall also have the right to inspect the records with respect to his own account and, in addition, shall be given any reports provided for by ERISA. Within sixty (60) days following the close of each Plan Year (or after the Trustee's removal or resignation pursuant to Section 10.3), the Trustee shall file with the Employer a written report or reports which shall indicate the receipts, disbursements, and other transactions for such year (or period ending with such resignation or removal) and the assets and liabilities of the Trust at its close.

(g) Returns and Reports. The Employer shall furnish to the Trustee, and the Trustee shall furnish to the Employer, such information relevant to the Trust as may be required under the Internal Revenue Code and Regulations issued or forms adopted thereunder. The Trustee shall keep such records, make such identification, and file with the Internal Revenue Service such returns and other information concerning the Trust as may be required of it under the Internal Revenue Code and Regulations issued or forms adopted thereunder.

(h) Voting Company Stock. The Trustee shall vote the Company Stock that it holds in Trust in accordance with instructions from the Committee as provided in Section 9.2(a). If the Committee shall fail or refuse to give the Trustee timely instructions, the power to vote such Company Stock shall pass to the Participants.

(i) Delivery of Materials Relating to Investments. The Trustee shall deliver or cause to be delivered to the Committee all notices, prospectuses, financial statements, proxies, and proxy soliciting materials relating to investments held for the Account of the Participants.

(j) Appointment of Agents. The Trustee shall have the power to employ such agents and counsel as may be reasonably necessary in collecting, managing, administering, investing, distributing, and protecting the Fund or the assets thereof and to pay them reasonable compensation. The counsel so retained may be counsel for the Employer.

The Trustee shall be fully protected in any action taken or not taken by it in good faith pursuant to advice or counsel of agents, and shall in no event be liable for the action or nonaction of such agents, provided the Trustee shall have exercised due care in selection of such agents.

(k) Investment of Trust Assets. The Trustee shall make only such investments as the Committee directs pursuant to Article XI.

(l) Interpretation of Plan Provisions. With the exception of those powers and duties specifically allocated to the Trustee by the express terms of this Plan, it shall not be the responsibility of the Trustee to interpret the terms of the Plan, and the Trustee may request, and is entitled to receive, guidance and written direction from the Committee on any point requiring construction or interpretation of Plan documents.

10.6 *Limitation of Liability.* The Trustee shall not be responsible for the purpose of propriety of any distribution made pursuant to Section 10.5(d) or any action or nonaction taken pursuant to the written instructions of the Committee. The Trustee shall not be responsible for any loss incurred with respect to any investment made or retained in accordance with the direction of the Committee. The Trustee shall be liable only for its own negligence or willful misconduct in failing to carry out such instructions received from the Committee, or its negligence or willful misconduct in the performance of the duties expressly conferred upon it under the Trust. The Trustee may conclusively rely upon, and shall not be liable to anyone for acting upon, any such written instruction, certification, notice, direction, or request, or any other instrument or paper believed by it to be genuine and to have been properly executed by any person authorized by the Committee to give instructions concerning the Trust.

10.7 *Multiple Trustees.* When two or more persons serve as Trustees, they are specifically authorized, by a written agreement between themselves, to allocate specific responsibilities, obligations, and duties among themselves. An original copy of such written agreement shall be delivered to the Employer and retained with other Plan documents.

The Trustees may delegate to one of their number the authority to sign documents, and the signature of any such authorized Trustee on any document shall be binding upon the Trust.

All decisions by the Trustees shall be made by the vote of the majority. A dissenting Trustee who, within a reasonable time after he has knowledge of any action or failure to act by the majority, registers his dissent in writing delivered to the other Trustees, the Employer, and the Committee shall not be responsible for any such action or failure to act.

ARTICLE XI. INVESTMENT OF TRUST ASSETS

11.1 *General Investment Policy.* The investment policy of the Plan is designed to invest primarily in Company Stock. All investments will be made by the Trustee only upon the direction of the Committee, and all purchases of Company Stock shall be made at prices that, in the judgment of the Committee, do not exceed the fair market value of such shares.

11.2 *Initial Acquisition of Company Stock.* The Trust shall acquire Company Stock by way of Employer Contributions, and/or the Trust shall acquire Company Stock at its fair market value with funds that the Trust possesses or will borrow. The loan will be repaid by the Trust to the lender on an installment basis over a period of years out of Employer Contributions.

The following provisions apply to such loans to the Trust:

(a) The loan must be at a reasonable rate of interest.

(b) Any collateral pledged to the lender by the Trust shall consist only of the assets purchased with the borrowed funds (although in addition to such collateral, the Employer may guarantee repayment of the loan).

(c) Under the terms of the loan, the lender shall have no recourse against the trust except with respect to such collateral.

(d) The loan shall be repaid only from those amounts contributed by the Employer to the Trust and from amounts earned on Trust investments.

(e) The Employer must contribute to the trust amounts sufficient to enable the trust to pay each installment of principal and interest on the loan on or before the date such installment is due, even if no tax benefit results from such contribution.

(f) Upon the payment of any portion of the balance due on

the loan, the assets originally pledged as collateral for such portion shall be released from encumbrance.

11.3 *Investment of Cash.* All Employer Contributions in cash and any other cash received by the Trust will first be used to pay current obligations of the Trust, and any excess will be used to buy Company Stock from holders of outstanding stock or newly issued stock from the Company. All purchases of Company Stock shall be made at a price, or at prices, which, in the judgment of the Committee, do not exceed the fair market value of such shares of Company Stock, except in cases when such purchase is made from a third party in accordance with Section 7.12. If no current obligations of the Trust are outstanding and unpaid, and the Committee determines that there is no company stock available for purchase, the Committee may direct the Trustee to invest funds of the Trust in savings accounts, bank certificates of deposit, high-grade short-term securities, or other equity stocks, bonds, or investments deemed by the Committee to be desirable for the Trust, or such funds may be held temporarily in cash.

11.4 *Key-Man Insurance.* The Committee may direct the Trustee to invest in life insurance policies on the lives of key employees of the Employer, payable on death to the Trust as Beneficiary. Such Policies shall be vested exclusively in the Trustee for the benefit of the Trust, and death proceeds received under any such Policies shall be allocated as specified in Section 5.3(d).

ARTICLE XII. AMENDMENT OR TERMINATION

12.1 *Amendment of Plan.* This Plan may be amended at any time by resolution of the Board. Written notice of any such amendment shall be given by the Employer to the Trustee. No amendment shall:

(a) deprive any Participant or Beneficiary of any of the benefits to which he is entitled under the Trust with respect to contributions previously made;

(b) make it possible for any part of the corpus or income of the Trust to be used for or diverted to purposes other than the exclusive benefit of the Participants or their Beneficiaries;

(c) expand or increase the duties or liabilities of the Trustee without its consent.

A copy of any such amendment shall be provided to the Trustee by the Employer.

12.2 *Amendment of Trust.* The Trustee and the Employer may enter into a supplemental agreement of trust solely with regard to the provisions of Article X for the purpose of modifying the powers, duties, immunities, or administration of the Trustee. Any such agreement shall be in a writing executed with the same formality as the Trust, and shall be deemed a part of the Trust as if the same were herein incorporated.

12.3 *Voluntary Termination.* This Plan may be completely or partially terminated at any time by resolution of the Board. No obligation to maintain or continue the Plan or contributions hereunder shall be implied. Such termination shall be effected by an instrument in writing delivered to the Trustee, and upon such termination all Accounts and interest shall become vested and nonforfeitable. The Trustee shall distribute to each Participant, former Participant, or Beneficiary of a Participant affected, any values credited to his Account or interest, contingent or fixed.

12.4 *Involuntary Termination.* The Trust shall terminate and distribution shall be made as provided in Section 12.3 if (a) the Employer is dissolved or adjudicated bankrupt or insolvent in appropriate proceedings, or if a general assignment is made by the Employer for the benefit of creditors, or (b) the Employer should lose its identity by merger, consolidation, or reorganization into one or more corporations or organizations, unless within sixty (60) days after such merger, reorganization, or consolidation, such corporations or organizations elect by an instrument in writing delivered to the Trustee to continue the Trust and such continuance is approved by the Trustee.

12.5 *Discontinuance of Contributions.* In the event that the Employer shall completely discontinue its contributions, each Participant, former Participant, or Beneficiary of a Participant affected shall be fully vested in any amounts credited to his Account as provided under Section 12.3. The Employer shall direct the Trustee in writing to make immediate distribution of the Trust assets or to make distribution in such form and under the circumstances that would have controlled such distributions if there had been no discontinuance of contributions.

12.6 *Merger or Consolidation of the Plan.* In the event of a merger or consolidation of this Plan with another qualified plan, or the transfer of the Plan assets or liabilities to another plan, the benefits a Participant is entitled to receive under this Plan shall not be reduced by such merger, consolidation, or transfer.

ARTICLE XIII. MISCELLANEOUS

13.1 *Section Headings.* The headings of this Plan have been inserted for convenience of reference only and are to be ignored in any construction of the provisions hereof.

13.2 *Nonguarantee of Employment.* Nothing herein contained shall be construed as giving any Participant the right to be retained in the service of the Employer, nor upon dismissal or upon his voluntary termination, to have any right or interest in this Plan other than as provided herein.

13.3 *Action by Employer.* Whenever under the terms of this Plan and the Trust created herein, the Employer is permitted or required to take some action, such action may be taken by an officer of the Employer who has been duly authorized by the Board.

13.4 *Nonalienation of Benefits.* Except as provided in Section 7.11, no right to receive benefits, nor any interest in this Plan and Trust, shall be subject to assignment, alienation, transfer, or anticipation, either by voluntary or involuntary act of any Participant or Beneficiary or by operation of law, nor shall such payment or right or interest be subject to the demands or claims of any creditor of such person, nor be liable in any way for such person's debts, obligations, or liabilities.

13.5 *Applicable Law: Invalidity of Provisions.* The validity of this Plan or any of its provisions shall be determined under and construed according to the laws of the state of Oregon. If any provision of this Plan shall be held illegal or invalid for any reason, such determination shall not affect the remaining provisions of this Plan and it shall be construed as if said illegal or invalid provision had never been included.

13.6 *Fiduciary Liability Insurance.* The Employer may obtain, pay for, and keep current a policy or policies of insurance insuring the Plan, the members of the Board, and members of the Committee and any other person to whom any fiduciary responsibility with respect to the Plan is allocated or delegated from, and against any and all liabilities, costs, and expenses incurred by such persons as a result of any act or omission to act in connection with the performance of their duties, responsibilities, and obligations under the Plan and under law.

13.7 *Participant's Benefits Limited to Trust Assets.* All Plan benefits will be paid only from the Trust assets, and neither the Employer, the Committee, nor the Trustee shall have any duty or liability to furnish the Trust with any funds, securities or other assets except as expressly provided in the Plan.

IN WITNESS WHEREOF, the Employer has caused this Plan and Trust Agreement to be signed by its duly authorized officers and the Trustee and members of the Committee signifying their acceptance of the responsibilities created herein have also signed this Plan and Trust Agreement.

ESOT Average, Inc.

Date: _____   By: _____

Title: _____

Date: _____   By: _____

Title: _____

Date: _____   By: _____

Title: _____

Committee Members

Date: _____   _____

Date: _____   _____

Date: _____   _____

Trustee:

Date: _____   _____

8

GENERAL SECURITIES REQUIREMENTS

An ESOP's security is generally without registration problems under federal securities laws if it is a noncontributory plan in which the employees have no say in the matter of distribution; therefore, no registration with the SEC is required. However, when shares are distributed from the trust, it may be necessary to file Form S-8 or an investment letter. It is therefore advisable that an ESOP provide an employee with the right to resell his stock to the trust. While it would be contrary to the avowed purpose of the plan to require an employee to sell his stock, where there is no ready market for the stock the employee should be given an available purchaser in the trust itself.

Employer contributions to an Employee Stock Ownership Plan may be in cash, stock, or other employer property, or in nonemployer securities. Usually, the contributions are in employer stock and cash. The cash may be accumulated to purchase employee-owned shares when participating employees terminate.

FEDERAL SECURITIES LAWS COVERING ESOPs

The Securities Act of 1933 makes it unlawful to sell or offer to sell a security utilizing the mail or interstate commerce except pursuant to a restoration statement and prospectus that meets the 1933 Act requirements. Generally speaking, interest in profit-sharing plans has been found to be security, although where the participant has full investment choice, the interest in the plan may not be a security. In an ESOP, no investment choice is generally involved; therefore, the underlying stock would constitute a security. The 1933 Act provides that a sale or offer to sell exists only if value is to be received. Historically and for practical reasoning, the SEC has taken the position that, in the absence of employee contributions, plan interests need not be registered because there is "no sale." The SEC takes the stand that the plan and stock are merely an incident of employment that the employee cannot control. In brief, therefore, for security and corporate planning purposes, a properly designed ESOP has protections from various methods of registration that other stock transactions cannot avoid.

Section 3(a)(2) of the 1933 Act exempts from its registration plan interests in a trust fund maintained by a bank in connection with a qualified pension, profit-sharing, or stock-bonus plan, except where an amount in excess of employee contributions may be invested to purchase employer securities. This Section is limited to plan interests and applies only when a bank is a trustee; therefore, its usefulness is limited.

Section 4(2) of the 1933 Act exempts from registration transactions by an issuer not involving any public offering. The private offering exemption is available without regard to Rule 146; however, factors that determine whether the issue is private or public are so unclear that abiding by Rule 146 is the only practical alternative. The factors that Section 4(2) lists as affecting the private/public determination include the number of offerees, the size of the offering, the relationship of the offerees to one another, the method of offering, the sophistication of the offerees, and finally, the offerees' access to pertinent information.

Rule 146 generally applies only to issuers, and it does not obviate the problem of integration (i.e., treating what the issuer regards as several distinct offerings as one single offering that, when so integrated, cannot meet any test for exemption). However, if no offer is made within six months before or six months after the claimed private offering, no integration will occur. The following conditions must be observed in order to adhere to Rule 146:

1. No general advertising or soliciting is permitted.
2. Offeree must have sufficient knowledge and experience to be able to evaluate the purchase, or the offeree must be able

to bear the economic risk of the purchase. At the time of sale, the issuer must reasonably believe that both the knowledge and ability-to-bear-risk requirements are met.

3. The offeree must either have access to prospectus-type information or be furnished with such information. Offeree must also be in a position to obtain information verifying the prospectus-type information.

4. The number of offerees (not purchasers) cannot exceed thirty-five.

5. Issuer must take reasonable care to preclude purchasers from acting as underwriters, i.e., generally it must preclude resales except pursuant to Rule 144.

Takeover and acquisition problems are not normally associated with closely held corporations. Such problems generally arise where management cannot control enough stock to prevent an outsider from obtaining either working or absolute control. In a true public company, this problem generally stems from diversification of shareholders. But closely held companies can have such problems when a large block of shares is held by individuals not active in the business. In such cases, an ESOP may provide an opportunity (1) to acquire stock from the outside shareholders, thus removing the threat, or (2) to purchase additional stock, diluting the extent of the interest of the outside shareholders.

There are securities problems in going private with an ESOP— but to go private means the corporation has been public. However, an ESOP can be used in closely held or unity controlled corporations to acquire minority interest or to solidify control—i.e., to effect a "freezeout." Although state laws will apply, the problems that confront publicly held companies in such situations (e.g., an implied representation to remain public, full disclosure in proxy statements, delisting problems) are not present when a nonpublic corporation uses an ESOP to acquire existing shares.[1] The business purpose rule would generally seem to be met in an ESOP context—for example, such purposes might include increased productivity, financing, etc. With a properly structured ESOP, it

---

1. Walter V. Stafford, ed., *Securities and Corporate Planning Considerations*, pp. 368–75.

should be possible in most cases to accomplish the elimination of a minority without violation of any fiduciary obligation of the majority.

ESOPs do have advantages for public companies seeking to go private. For example, they can provide an excellent tender offer vehicle because any cash payment is in effect made on a tax-free basis. This permits flexibility in pricing not normally available. In addition, there is much interest by Congress in a purchase by and for employees under a tax-qualified plan, which by definition does not discriminate.

SUMMARY

The advantages and disadvantages of an ESOP as relating to other employee-benefit plans can be summarized in a discussion of degree of risk. While both the profit-sharing plan and the ESOP are capital-accumulation plans, the fact that an ESOP invests primarily in employer securities and may subject trust funds to capital-financing risk causes the ESOP to have the benefits of both a finance company and a stock-ownership entity. The value of this benefit to both employer and employees depends upon the performance of company stock and the timing of capital financing.

This summary reviews the pluses and minuses of a qualified plan that particularly relate to how the company,' the stockholders, and the employees share in the amenities that come from a properly designed trust. Corporate officers, directors, principal shareholders, and their advisers should be aware of the availability of this unique financial plan in order to determine if it can be advantageously programmed.

ESOPs' Yea-Yeas and Nay-Nays

The ESOP plan and design envisions the eventual sharing of ownership of the corporate entity by those that help produce the corporate income. The first question a prospective company should consider relates to the consequences to present stockholders, and perhaps the management of the company, regarding the control necessary to make and/or carry out past, present, and future corporate policies. Obviously, if the stock is widely held, there would appear no reasonable objections concerning dilution of ownership. The closely held company, however, must weigh the dilution of ownership against the advantages of leveraging the corporate pretax dollar and the benefits that would result from sharing stock with its employees.

The Internal Revenue Service requires that an ESOP be organized and designed to distribute stock to its employee participants. Consequently, there is no simple way to permit the management to impose various restrictions upon the shares acquired by an employee—such as demanding that the employee sell the shares back to the company or to the ESOP trustee. A call provision in favor of management or the trust could effectively deny an employee his rights concerning stock ownership, thereby annulling the intent and purpose of the ESOP design. The right of refusal may be attached to the securities so long as the agreement providing for this arrangement stipulates that the price of the stock to be paid to the employee shall not be less than its fair market value. In no event shall the employer offer a price less than the price offered to the employee by another potential buyer making a bona fide offer.

It is acceptable for the employee to negotiate a put to the company, since this does not restrict ownership of the stock. Furthermore, the put may be at a predetermined or formula price, since the exercise of this kind of option is at the sole discretion of the former employee who has possession of the stock. Properly designed, a put could be programmed either to the corporation or to the trust in order to assure the retiring employee that there is a market for his stock. However, the IRS Pension Trust Department personnel governing approval of plans presently take the position that to put a stock to the trust might violate ERISA requirements regarding prudent investments if the trustee were bound to purchase the stock at a time that he might consider inappropriate.

The corporation that has formed the ESOP has the right to contribute various classes of stock that do not carry the same voting rights; therefore, these options are available should management desire to consolidate control or to regulate the stock's redemption qualities. A disadvantage of issuing more than one type of stock is that the valuation process may become more complicated, since one type of stock may have more value than another. In court cases, voting and nonvoting stocks have been given different values for estate tax purposes; the company designing the plan should take this into consideration in valuation procedures.

As an estate-planning tool, an ESOP has wide ramifications.

The Employee Stock Ownership Trust can be a market for shares of a majority stockholder's stock, either during his lifetime or after his death. Frequently, controlling shareholders desire to sell a part of their shares in order to diversify their holdings or to provide liquidity for investment or estate-planning purposes. Usually, however, there is no market for the sale of a minority interest in a closely held company. The ESOP solves part of this problem by providing an available market for the purchase of shares from controlling shareholders—simultaneously enabling the shareholder to derive favorable capital gains rates. Flexibility is available in structuring stock sales to the ESOP. Combining an installment sale and a serial sale permits certain financial advantages to a shareholder that might otherwise be lost: in a serial sale, the stockholder disposes of some shares each year and benefits from any price appreciation—which is not permitted in a strict installment sale agreement.

The ESOP provides a readily available market for the venture capitalist, the investment banker, the minority shareholder, and other outside investors who desire to realize their capital gain or to liquidate a part of their investment for reinvestment purposes.

The venture capitalist and the investment banker have realized and are accepting the fact that an ESOP increases the company's ability to attract and retain highly skilled management technicians, thereby making their own investment more secure. The incentive provided by an ESOP is usually superior to that resulting from other kinds of plans.

An ESOP must be wisely designed in order to protect and maintain corporate control by its existing management. When the ESOT holds a majority of the stock, the employer can vote this stock through the trustee. If the ESOT possesses only a minority interest, the trustee can align himself with other minority interests and perhaps establish a majority. However, even though the ESOT's provisions allow the board of directors to select trustees at their pleasure and discretion, the IRS may well take the position that friendly selectivity regarding a trustee may not primarily benefit employees. This can definitely be a nay-nay if the trust is not designed to show that company management will always be a factor that is in harmony with, but not a vehicle to take over, the regulation/control of the trust. The designs and plans that are acceptable to the Pension Trust Review Department do permit a plan to have "guardrails" assuring perpetuity of control to management; thoughtful consideration should be given to avoiding a potential nay-nay position in this regard.

The corporation that is considering an ESOP should first appraise its objectives and capabilities before formulating a plan. The company must be willing to give, and the employees to accept, stock of the corporation before an ESOP can be of practical value. The preliminary study requires providing an understandable explanation to management as well as other personnel; therefore, an initial review is expensive. Once the preliminary plan has been accepted by management, the administrative costs are similar to those of profit-sharing plans. The larger the payroll base, the larger the allowable deductions to the ESOP. Any net operating loss that results can be carried back and forward to recover taxes. But these characteristics, although important, are not the leading features of the analytical work that is necessary to determine whether or not an ESOP should be adopted by any particular corporation.

The corporation considering an ESOP should determine how its own state security law relates to the restoration statement of an Employee Stock Ownership Plan proposal. States have different rulings regarding plans and designs; therefore, your legal department should investigate not only federal security laws but also pertinent state laws and regulations. The privately held company must weigh the cost of forming an ESOP in relationship to the expected return. No wise investor today invests in any program without considering the yeas and nays of dollars invested. Registering the ESOP participation can be costly; therefore, the preliminary study should determine whether the corporation has a registration problem.

Companies without labor unions have been more interested in ESOPs than those with unions, the reason being that some company owners view the ESOP as a means of making it less likely that their workers will join a union. They feel that employees, having been given a "piece of the action," will have second thoughts about joining a union. This view, however, is a secondary rather than the primary reason for implementing a plan. The unionization of workers is quite complete in many industries throughout the nation; however, a design can include the union personnel or exclude them. Because most unions presently have a retirement plan, ERISA permits a plan to be designed with or without the inclusion of union personnel.

Generally, an ESOP is structured to give employees a noncontributory interest; hence, the source of an ESOP fund is totally employer contributions. Plans and designs can be structured for employee contribution, but then registration problems and SEC problems immediately come into play. The federal law specifically gives tax-exempt status to employee participation in qualified stock-bonus plans unless "an amount in excess of the employer's contribution" is used to purchase employer securities. The major reason for not having employees make contributions to an ESOP trust is an administrative ruling that gives tax-exempt status to *employer* contributions to a qualified plan that uses no employee contributions to acquire employer stock. Borrowing funds from a lender to purchase corporate stock also has this exempt status, since the employer contribution in the future will go to pay for all shares that are distributed to the participants.

A disgruntled employee-participant who, after leaving his employment, does not wish to sell his stock to the trust or the corporation could give management problems at annual meetings and in other corporate programs. He will be a stockholder of the company entitled to stockholder's rights as permitted under federal and state regulations and laws. This employee-participant who may be dissatisfied with company operations has the right to challenge the company concerning corporate accounting, and if misappropriations were proven, the company would be in an adverse situation.

The most tested method of dealing with problems of minority shareholders is through buy-back arrangements under which the employer company or the ESOT can buy back distributed stock from an employee beneficiary or his estate. A mandatory buy-back arrangement cannot be created by the company, since this would disqualify the trust as a tax-exempt employee trust. However, a provision giving the employee-beneficiary an option to sell his stock to the company or trust, if he so desires, is not in conflict with this requirement, and such provisions in stock-bonus plans have been satisfactory to the Internal Revenue Service.

ESOP-sponsoring companies now have track records to prove success through higher employee productivity, and they are finding the dollar-leverage factor increasingly desirable. Properly planned and organized, this unique financial design will afford the corporation, the key executives, and the shareholders a greater sense of balance and harmony. To understand the impetus toward ESOP-favoring legislation by politicians in influential positions, consider the following facts:

1. Production, to be competitive, must function with two factors—labor and capital.
2. Affluence is the product of capital only when dollars diffuse meaningfully through capital ownership.
3. Capital can be financed easily and logically from credit if new capital owners and new capital are formed at the same time.

9

EMPLOYEE
STOCK OWNERSHIP PLAN
ACCOUNTING PROCEDURES
MANUAL

The ESOP's trust committee is charged with the overall responsibility concerning the plan's general accounting rules and practices. The committee's objective is to assure the company employees who have stock interest in the trust that proper books of account are maintained and regularly audited.

This chapter considers the allocation/ownership aspects of the stock that is annually credited to the participants' accounts. What to do about dividends, who shares in the net income (or loss) of the trust, and accounting for distributions is explained and discussed.

To assure the proper discharge of its responsibility and to accomplish its objectives, the trust committee should be thoroughly knowledgeable regarding the rules and policies contained in the company's ESOP accounting manual.

The accounting procedures outlined below are designed to provide rules and guidelines for use in recording—

1. the various transactions of the Employee Stock Ownership Plan (ESOP), and
2. the interests of the Participants in the Trust, pursuant to Article V, 5.3(c) (see chapter 7).

Part I of the manual sets forth the general accounting rules for recording contributions and allocations where there is no financing or other obligations of the trust involved. Part II of the manual sets forth rules to cover situations where there is debt financing or other obligations incurred by the trust in connection with the purchase of company stock. The accounting for distributions to participants for all situations is covered in Part I.

Throughout this manual, the definitions of terms and the provisions of the ESOP set forth in chapter 7 will be assumed. Additional definitions are provided in the manual as required.

PART I. GENERAL ACCOUNTING RULES

A. TRUST ACCOUNTS

1. *Balance Sheet Accounts.* The Trust's balance sheet accounts for Trust assets should include a Company Stock Fund and an Other Investments Fund, each maintained in dollars and cents. They are designed to record the value of assets (Company stock, cash, and other property) received, held, and disbursed by the Trust.

   a) Company Stock Fund. The Company Stock Fund will reflect the value of Company stock acquired by the Trust. In the case of a purchase of Company stock for cash or other property, such value will be the actual cost of the shares. In the case of a contribution of Company stock from the Company, such value will be the fair market value of the shares, as determined by the Committee, at the time that the shares are actually issued to the Trust.

   b) Other Investments Fund. The Other Investments Fund will reflect the fair market value of any Employer contributions in cash and the fair market value of receipts attributable to assets credited to the Other Investments Fund. As of each Anniversary Date, the Other Investments Fund will be valued at the fair market value of all its assets.

   The balances in these Funds must be adjusted to reflect receipt and disbursement, including distribution, of Trust assets.

2. *Non-Balance Sheet Accounts.* The accounts described below are not balance sheet accounts of the Trust. They are

designed to reflect the value of Trust assets prior to allocation to the accounts of Participants.

   a) *Unallocated Company Stock Account.* This account,
   maintained in shares of Company stock, will be initially
   credited with all shares of Company stock received by
   the Trust. This applies to all shares of Company stock
   regardless of how they are acquired by the Trust,
   whether by contribution from the Company or by purchase from the Company or shareholders (including
   former Participants). As of each Anniversary Date,
   certain shares of company stock will be transferred out
   of this Account and allocated to the Participants' Company Stock Accounts, as described below.

   b) *Unallocated Other Investments Account.* This account,
   maintained in dollars and cents, will be initially credited
   with the fair market value of all cash and other assets
   received by the Trust. It will be debited with any payments in unallocated cash or other assets from the
   Other Investments Fund. As of each Anniversary Date,
   the total balance of this Account will be debited and
   allocated to Participants' Other Investments Accounts
   as described below.

B. PARTICIPANTS' ACCOUNTS
   1. *Company Stock Account.* A Company Stock Account is
   established for each Participant. It reflects the number of
   shares of Company stock that have been allocated to the
   Participant. The number of shares shall be uniformly recorded in either hundredths or thousandths of a share.
   2. *Other Investments Account.* An Other Investments Account is established for each Participant. It is valued in
   dollars and cents and reflects the fair market value of cash
   and other assets of the Trust (other than Company stock)
   allocated to that Participant as of each Anniversary Date.

C. ANNUAL ALLOCATIONS TO PARTICIPANTS' ACCOUNTS
   All Company stock received by the Trust will initially be
   credited to the Unallocated Company Stock Account. The
   value of all other assets received by the Trust will be credited
   to the Unallocated Other Investments Account. (The trust
   funds, described in Section A, reflecting the balance sheet accounts of the Trust, should also reflect these receipts.) As of

each Anniversary Date, the amounts in these accounts will be allocated to Participants' Accounts as follows:

1. *Employer Contributions*

   a) Employer Contributions in Company stock are allocated to Participants' Company Stock Accounts in accordance with the allocation formula in Article V of the ESOP [see chapter 7].

   b) Employer Contributions in cash are allocated to Participants' Other Investments Accounts in accordance with the allocation formula in Article V, 5.3, Allocations, of the ESOP [see chapter 7].

2. *Forfeitures*

   a) To determine the amount forfeited by a terminated Participant, the following steps should be taken:

   (1) Determine the value of the Company stock in that Participant's Company Stock Account by multiplying the current fair market value per share by the number of shares.

   (2) This amount plus the current balance in his Other Investments Account gives the total value of the Participant's account balances.

   (3) Multiply the total value of his account balances by the percentage that is not vested to compute the amount of the Forfeiture (under the vesting schedule of Article VII, 7.4 of the ESOP) [see chapter 7].

   (4) The Forfeiture should be charged to the Other Investments Account balance to the extent thereof. If the Forfeiture exceeds the Other Investments Account balance, the balance of the Forfeiture will be charged to the Company Stock Account.

   b) The Forfeiture of balances from Participants' Other Investments Accounts is allocated to the Other Investments Accounts of remaining Participants, as described in Article V, 5.3 of the ESOP [see chapter 7].

   c) The Forfeiture of shares of Company stock from Participants' Company Stock Accounts is allocated to the remaining Participants, as described in Article V, 5.3 of the ESOP [see chapter 7].

3. *Dividends on Company Stock*

a) Cash dividends received during a year on shares of Company stock that have been allocated to Participants' Company Stock Accounts will be credited to the respective Participants' Other Investments Accounts.

b) Cash dividends received during a year on shares of Company stock in the Unallocated Company Stock Account will be added to the Trust net income (or loss) and allocated to Participants' Other Investments Accounts as provided in Subsection 4 below.

c) Stock dividends received during a year on shares of Company stock that have been allocated to Participants' Company Stock Accounts will be credited to the respective Participants' Company Stock Accounts.

d) Stock dividends received during a year on shares of Company stock in the Unallocated Company Stock Account will be credited to the Unallocated Company Stock Account and allocated in the same manner as the shares with respect to which they were received.

e) If cash dividends are distributed to Participants by the Trust (in accordance with Article VII of the ESOP) [see chapter 7], the amount of the distribution will be debited to the respective Participants' Other Investments Accounts.

4. *Net Income (or Loss) of the Trust*

a) The net income (or loss) of the Trust (attributable to Employer Contributions) will be computed annually as of the Anniversary Date. Net income (or loss) includes the increase (or decrease) in the fair market value of the assets of the Trust (other than Company stock), interest income, dividends (other than on allocated Company stock), and other income (or loss) of the Trust, less any expenses of the Trust that are not paid by the Company. It does not include any interest paid on a loan used by the Trust to purchase Company stock or under an installment contract for the purchase of Company stock.

b) As of each Anniversary Date, the amount of the net income (or loss) will be allocated to the Participants' Other Investments Accounts in proportion to the relative account balances on the preceding Anniversary

Date (reduced by any distribution), as provided in Article V, 5.3(c) of the ESOP [see chapter 7].

D. ALLOCATING CASH PURCHASES OF
COMPANY STOCK BY TRUST

The following rules apply where there is no debt incurred for the purchase of Company stock. Part II of the manual sets forth rules to cover situations where there are debt obligations (including loans and installment purchases) incurred by the Trust in connection with the purchase of company stock.

Shares of Company stock purchased by the Trust with cash must be allocated to the Participants' Company Stock Accounts. The determination of how to allocate such shares will depend upon the source of the funds used to purchase the Company stock.

1. Where purchases are made from current Employer Contributions of cash, the procedures below should be followed.

   a) Employer Contributions of cash should be allocated and credited to the Other Investments Accounts of Participants as provided in Section C1*b* above. This allocation should be made as of the particular Anniversary Date, prior to recording the purchase of company stock, irrespective of whether the purchase is made prior to or after the Anniversary Date.

   b) The amount of the purchase price that is paid by the Trust should be debited to the Other Investments Accounts of the Participants in the same proportions as the Employer Contribution was allocated, as described above. This will reduce the Other Investments Accounts of all Participants for the amount of cash (or other property) disbursed by the Trust.

   c) The number of shares of Company stock purchased by the Trust should then be credited to the Company Stock Accounts of the Participants in the same proportions as the debit for the payment was allocated to their Other Investments Accounts.

2. Where purchases are made from amounts previously allocated to Participants' Other Investments Accounts, the procedures below should be followed.

   a) The purchase price will be debited to the Other Investments Accounts of Participants in proportion to those account balances on the preceding Anniversary Date (reduced by the amount of any distribution during the year).

b) The number of shares of Company stock purchased by the Trust should be credited to the Company Stock Accounts of the Participants in the same proportions as the debits for the payment were allocated to their Other Investments Accounts.

3. Where purchases are made partly from a current Employer Contribution and partly from existing assets of the Trust, or where the source for the purchases is unclear, the Committee should account for the purchases on the basis that most nearly reflects the actual origin of the funds.

In all cases, adjustments in the Trust Fund balances should be made to reflect the changes in the Trust, as provided in Section A1 above.

E. ACCOUNTING FOR DISTRIBUTIONS

1. The distribution of a Participant's Capital Accumulation *must* be in shares of Company stock (except for the value of fractional shares) as required by Article VII of the ESOP [see chapter 7]. Where a Participant's Capital Accumulation includes a balance in his Other Investments Account, such balance must be used to acquire shares of Company stock for distribution. This generally will be done as a bookkeeping matter within the Trust, as described below.

2. The Participant's Other Investments Account will be debited for the full amount of the credit balance thereof. Said amount will be credited to the Unallocated Other Investments Account.

3. A number of shares of Company stock, equal in value to the Participant's Other Investments Account balance, will be credited to said Participant's Company Stock Account and distributed as part of his Capital Accumulation. The value of the shares of Company stock will be the fair market value, as determined by the Committee, on the Anniversary Date as of which the Capital Accumulation is computed.

4. The shares credited to the Participant's Company Stock Account will come from one of the following sources:

a) If there are shares in the Unallocated Company Stock Account, that account should be debited for the number of shares. In this case, the credit for the Other Investments Account balance that would be made to the Unallocated Other Investments Account, pursuant to Subsection 2 above, would be allocated to Participants in the same manner as the shares of Company stock would have otherwise been allocated.

b) If there are no shares of Company stock in the Unallocated Company Stock Account, the shares must come from Company stock contributed or forfeited that year, prior to allocation of the remainder to other Participants under Section C2 above.

5. If sufficient shares of Company stock are not available from either the Unallocated Company Stock Account or from current Employer Contributions or Forfeitures to credit the Participant's Company Stock Account, as provided in Subsection 3 above, the Trust should acquire (or borrow) additional shares from the Company or from shareholders (including former Participants) to the extent that they are available. However, any remaining balance in a Participant's Other Investments Account attributable to amounts transferred from a profit-sharing plan may be distributed in cash.

6. If shares of Company stock distributed to a Participant (or Beneficiary) are repurchased in accordance with Article VII of the ESOP [see chapter 7], the repurchase shall be accounted for as a cash purchase under Section D above, or a financed purchase under Part II, as the case may be.

F. Stock Splits and Capital Reorganizations

Any Company stock received by the Trust as the result of a stock split or any reorganization or recapitalization of the Company shall be credited to the account to which the Company stock affected is credited.

G. Fractional Shares

If a Participant's Capital Accumulation includes a fractional share of Company stock at the time that a distribution is called for under the Plan, the fair market value of such fractional share, as determined by the Committee, shall be transferred from the Unallocated Other Investments Account to the Participant's Other Investments Account and distributed in cash. The fractional share shall be transferred from the Participant's Company Stock Account to the Unallocated Company Stock Account.

PART II. FINANCED PURCHASE OF COMPANY STOCK

A. IN GENERAL

The rules contained in this Part cover situations where the Trust purchases shares of Company stock and the purchase price is paid (1) with the proceeds of a loan to the Trust, (2) in installments pursuant to a stock purchase or other agreement, or (3) in any combination thereof. All purchases of Company stock paid for in this manner shall be referred to as "financed purchases" of Company stock. The shares of Company stock will initially be offset by the amount of the debt, and the Participants will not have an equity in the shares. Accordingly, while the shares should be credited to the Company Stock Fund, with a corresponding debt in a liability account to record the Trust's liability for financed purchases, the shares are not allocated to the Participants' accounts at that time. The purpose of this Part II is to set forth rules for the allocation of such shares to the Company Stock Accounts of the Participants as the debt is paid off.

B. INITIAL ALLOCATION UPON PURCHASE OF
COMPANY STOCK

1. Where shares of Company stock are acquired entirely as a financed purchase, all of the shares shall be credited initially to the Unallocated Company Stock Account.

2. Where shares of Company stock are acquired (1) in part with a down payment out of funds in the Trust (including current Employer Contributions) and (2) in part as a financed purchase, the total number of shares of Company stock purchased shall be allocated proportionately between the two categories. The number of shares of Company stock fully paid for out of existing Trust funds shall be allocated to Company Stock Accounts as provided in Section D of Part I (General Accounting Rules). The number of shares acquired as a financed purchase shall be credited initially to the Unallocated Company Stock Account.

C. ALLOCATION FROM UNALLOCATED
COMPANY STOCK ACCOUNT

In case of a financed purchase of Company stock, as the Trust pays a part or all of the debt (principal and interest), a part or all of the Company stock in the Unallocated Company Stock Account is allocated and credited to the Company Stock Accounts of the Participants. The following rules will apply:

1. The allocation of Employer Contributions, Forfeitures, and net income (or loss) shall be recorded as of the Anniversary Date on which they are determined. All other transactions are recorded as of the Anniversary Date after they occur. For example, an Employer Contribution in cash for one year may be actually received by the Trust and used to pay a part of the debt in the following year. The cash contribution would be allocated to the Participants' Other Investments Accounts as of the Anniversary Date of the first year. The payment on the debt and the allocation of Company stock to the Participants' Company Stock Accounts would be recorded as of the Anniversary Date of the second year.

2. As of the Anniversary Date of a year during which payments are made on the debt, the shares that are thereby deemed to be purchased and paid for by the Trust are allocated to Participants' Company Stock Accounts. The number of shares that shall be released from the Unallocated Company Stock Account shall be determined by multiplying the total number of shares acquired in the particular financed purchase by the following fraction:

   a) The numerator is the amount of all debt payments made during that year (including principal *and* interest).

   b) The denominator is the total amount of all payments made and to be made on the entire debt (including principal *and* interest) incurred for that financed purchase.

   The product of multiplying this fraction by the number of shares acquired as a financed purchase will be the number of shares of Company stock to be allocated to the Participants' Company Stock Accounts for the particular year based upon the repayment of debt.

3. Where the interest rate is fixed, the total interest over the term of the financing is readily determinable. Where the interest rate fluctuates, the foregoing formula shall be followed, except that, in computing the number of shares to be released in connection with payments made following the change in interest rates, all payments made and shares allocated in years prior to the change in interest shall thereafter be excluded from the formula so that (1) the numerator shall be calculated as before, (2) the denominator shall exclude payments made prior to the interest rate change and shall be based in part upon a projection of the total interest cost assuming the new interest rate remains constant for the remainder of the repayment period, and (3) the multiplicand shall include only those shares not previously allocated during the terms of prior interest rates.

4. If additional debt is incurred to meet payments on the original financed purchase, the number of shares which shall be released from the Unallocated Company Stock Account shall be determined by multiplying the unallocated shares remaining from the original financed purchase by the following fraction:

   a) The numerator is the amount of payments made during that year (including principal *and* interest) less any proceeds of the new debt applied toward payments on the original debt.

   b) The denominator is the total debt payments made that year and to be made (including principal *and* interest) on the original debt, less any proceeds of the new debt applied toward payments on the original debt, plus the total amount of the payments made and to be made on the new debt.

5. Any payments made by the Trust under a financed purchase of Company stock will be debited to the Participants' Other Investments Accounts for each Participant's allocable share of the payment. The debts to the Other Investments Accounts will be allocated among the Participants according to the source of the funds used to make the payment (see Section D of Part I). Where the source of funds is Employer Contributions, the Other Investments Accounts

will be debited in the same proportions as Employer Contributions were allocated to these accounts initially.

6. The number of shares of Company stock released from the Unallocated Company Stock Account, as determined in Subsection 2, 3, or 4 above, shall be allocated and credited to the Participants' Company Stock Accounts in the same proportions as their Other Investments Accounts are debited, pursuant to Subsection 5 above.

10

DESCRIPTIVE EMPLOYEE

HANDBOOK

An Employee Stock Ownership Plan is designed to provide employees with the incentive of "a piece of the action" and to enable them to share in the capital growth of the company. Employee stock plans give employees a direct and vested interest in the success of the company, share with them profits of their own labor, and form a workable interest between management and labor.

People (labor) must produce wealth by either making goods or offering services, and there is no easy path for a company to follow regarding profit/production standards. It is sound reasoning to understand and accept the fact that the small to medium-size company can best compete with the large multinational corporations by taking on a genuine concern for employees. Employees are a company's greatest asset. The data described in this chapter illustrate such genuineness.

ESOT AVERAGE, INC.:
EMPLOYEE STOCK OWNERSHIP AND
TRUST AGREEMENT

Congratulations!
You are buying yourself a corporation—your company—
ESOT Average, Inc.
And you are buying it the right way: so it will pay for itself
—without payroll deductions, and
—without cutting into your savings.

Provided...
—you work hard
—you work efficiently
—you hold down Company costs.

Following is a description of our ESOT Average, Inc., Employee Stock Ownership and Trust Agreement, which has made this purchase possible. The Plan under discussion is a combination Employee Stock Ownership Plan and Money Purchase Pension Plan (hereinafter referred to as an ESOP).

Part I: What Is the Retirement Plan and Trust Agreement of ESOT Average, Inc., and What Can It Do for You?

What Happened? ESOT Average, Inc., has adopted an Employee Stock Ownership Plan and Trust Agreement—the ESOP—a combination Employee Stock Ownership Plan and Money Purchase Pension Plan.

Under the ESOP you become a stockholder, an owner, entitled to benefits of ownership in addition to pay. As you work for the Company, you will build up a capital estate, invested primarily in Company stock, which can earn money even when you are not working. The size of your ESOP account will grow with your years in the Company and with the worth of the Company. As the Company prospers, you will share in the prosperity.

With those benefits comes a special responsibility to your fellow employee-owners and your Company. Company profitability increases the value of your ownership interest; poor management, inefficiency, and waste diminish it. No one has a stronger interest in caring for and promoting the business of a Company than its owners. That's the whole idea of our ESOP—as co-owners, we can all see the mutual benefit of doing just that. As an employee-owner, your stake in the Company, and the Company's stake in you, have significantly increased. This employee-ownership can only help to enhance the well-being of the Company and your interest in it.

In the long run, your Company will prosper as we all make it prosper; and that prosperity will quite literally be yours.

How Does This New Ownership Relationship Benefit Me? This Plan is an arrangement that allows you to build up capital by acquiring a share of the capital ownership of ESOT Average, Inc.,

(1) without any deductions from your paychecks, and (2) without any investment of your personal savings.

To accomplish this, the Company has set up an ESOP Trust that can receive tax-deductible contributions from the Company to finance the purchase of Company stock on your behalf using Company credit. In this way, the ESOP can buy Company stock for you and pay for it out of future earnings of the Company. You are in no way liable if any loan obligations are not met by the ESOP.

Of course, an ESOP is not the only device used today to connect employees to corporate earnings. Some companies have installed profit-sharing plans that accumulate for employees, while they are employed, a share of the Company's profits for distribution on termination of employment. However, under an ESOP, employees share not only in company earnings, but also in company ownership itself. Rather than simply a temporary share in the Company's profits, an ESOP gives to its participants a share of the corporate finance: the privilege to buy income-producing property out of the future income it produces, without personal financial risk.

In starting ESOT Average, Inc., and building its success, no one person did it all. At every level of job responsibility, the efforts and devotion of many individuals created the success we have achieved so far. The ESOP program of building employee *ownership* is an especially appropriate way to recognize these contributions.

Generally, How Does the Plan Work? Once each year, the Company will make contributions to the ESOP in Company stock, cash, or other property, as determined by the Company's Board of Directors. The contributions will be invested by the ESOP Trustee in Company stock and other investments exclusively for the benefit of the participating employees. The ESOP will purchase Company stock at prices that do not exceed the fair market value as determined under rules of the Internal Revenue Service. The ESOP may borrow to do this. If it does borrow, the loan will be backed by the Company's credit. At a minimum, the Company will contribute enough to the ESOP to satisfy any debt obligations incurred to purchase Company stock. Employees will not be required to pledge to repay the loan or to assume any other personal financial risk.

All Company stock contributed to the ESOP and all Company

stock purchased under the ESOP will be allocated annually to the accounts of Participants according to a formula related to their Covered Compensation (as defined in Part II of this booklet).

What Guarantees Are There that the Value of My Account Will Increase? There are never any guarantees that investments, even investments in your own Company, will increase. Prices tend to fluctuate. Frequently the averages on the public stock markets have dropped, despite good performances of many of the companies involved. However, the ESOP provides you with an investment more directly related to the quality of your performance and more shielded from the erratic changes of the public market. When the relationship between the value of Company stock and good employee motivation is reinforced by direct employee-ownership benefits, the chances for Company profitability can only be increased.

What Are the Tax Advantages of an ESOP? Payments by the Company to the ESOP are tax deductible by the Company within the limits of the Internal Revenue Code. This tax benefit enables you, through the ESOP, to acquire ownership of Company stock through the use of Company "before-tax" dollars instead of your own "aftertax" dollars. With combined federal and state corporate income tax rates generally approaching 50 percent, proper use of our ESOP will nearly double the power of this investment dollar. Thus the ESOP unites the interests of the Company and its employee-owners by allowing the Company to finance its growth at the same time that it finances your ownership in that growth, and to do it all with pretax dollars.

Further, you are not taxed on Company Contributions or your interest in the ESOP until it is distributed to you.

These and other tax aspects of the ESOP are discussed more fully in Part II of this booklet.

How Do I Find Out More About the ESOT Average, Inc., ESOP? Part II of this booklet, "Summary Plan Description," may answer additional questions you may have. From time to time, you will be receiving bulletins and announcements, as well as an annual statement of your account. *There are also copies of the Plan, Trust, and related documents on file at our principal business offices as listed in "Summary Plan Description." You may examine these documents at any time during our business hours. If you* have further questions, you should write to the ESOP Committee at our executive offices or talk with a member of the Committee. The names of the Committee members are set forth in Part II.

Part II: Summary Plan Description of the ESOT Average, Inc., Employee Stock Ownership Plan and Trust Agreement

What Does the Plan Mean to Me? ESOT Average, Inc., Employee Stock Ownership Plan and Trust Agreement (ESOP) has been adopted to enable the qualified employees of ESOT Average, Inc., to acquire capital ownership in ESOT Average, Inc. (the Company). Through increasing ownership of Company stock, the goal of the ESOP is to provide you with a meaningful stake in the Company, with future economic security, and ultimately with a second source of income.

The ESOP is designed to accomplish these objectives without taking money out of your paycheck or your savings, and without your being currently taxed on the value of stock acquisitions.

What Type of ESOP Is It? Your Company's ESOP is a retirement plan designed to qualify for special tax treatment under Section 401(a) of the Internal Revenue Code. The Plan is a combination Employee Stock Ownership Plan and Money Purchase Pension Plan.

Generally, How Does the ESOP Work? Once each year, the Company will make contributions to the ESOP in Company stock, cash, or other property, as determined by its Board of Directors. The contributions will be invested by the ESOP Trustee in Company stock and other investments exclusively for the benefit of participating employees. The ESOP will purchase Company stock at prices that do not exceed the fair market value as determined under the rules of the Internal Revenue Service. The ESOP may borrow to do this. If it does borrow, the loan will be backed by the Company's credit. At a minimum, the Company will contribute enough to the ESOP to satisfy any obligations incurred to purchase Company stock. Employees will not be required to pledge to repay the loan or to assume any other personal risk.

All Company stock contributed to the ESOP and all Company stock purchased under the ESOP will be allocated to the accounts of Participants, according to a formula related to their salaries.

Who Is Eligible to Participate? All employees of the Company as of October 1, 1975, who completed at least 1,000 hours of service in the twelve-month period that ended on September 30, 1975, shall be eligible to participate in this Plan as of the Effective Date (October 1, 1975). Every other employee will become a Participant in this Plan on the semiannual entry date next following his attainment of age twenty-five and the earlier of (a) the twelve-month period following his employment by Employer if he completes 1,000 hours of service during the period, or (b) the first Plan Year in which he completes 1,000 hours of service.

How Long Will My Participation Continue? Participation continues with service until it is terminated by death, retirement, Disability, or a "Break in Service"—i.e., a Plan Year in which a Participant fails to complete at least one Hour of Service.

It includes all periods of such employment with the Company, both before and after adoption of this Plan. If you return to work on or before the end of an authorized Leave of Absence, your service is not broken by the absence. Failure to return to work as a full-time employee on or before the end of an Authorized Leave of Absence will terminate service as of the beginning of the authorized Leave of Absence.

Who Pays for the Plan? Your Company will make annual contributions to the ESOP. Voluntary employee contributions are not permitted. Employees cannot contribute to the ESOP.

What Will the Company Contribute to the ESOP? The Employer will contribute to the Trust an amount as follows: For all Plan Years—(1) 10 percent of all Participants' Covered Compensation, plus (2) such amount (not to exceed 15 percent of all Participants' Covered Compensation) as may be determined by Board resolution adopted on or before the last day of the Plan Year. In the absence of such a resolution, the amount to be contributed under part (2) shall be 15 percent of Covered Compensation. However, the Employer contribution for each year shall never be less than the amount required to enable the Trust to discharge its current obligations.

Contributions will be made in Company stock, cash, or other property as determined by the Company's Board of Directors.

How Will Company Contributions and Other Trust Assets Be Invested? The assets of the ESOP traceable to Company Contributions will be held primarily in Company stock. Company Contributions in cash or other property will generally be used to purchase Company stock directly from the Company. However, the ESOP may also invest in assets other than Company stock or retain contributions in cash.

What Will Be My Share of Company Contributions? As of the thirtieth day of September of each year, your share of the Company's annual contributions will be allocated to your accounts. The allocation is computed as follows:

1. The Employer Contributions for each Trust Year shall be allocated among the accounts of Participants in accordance with the following formula:

   Employer contributions will be allocated as of each September 30th among the accounts of Participants so entitled in the ratio in which the Covered Compensation of each bears to the aggregate Covered Compensation of all Participants for that year.

2. Amounts forfeited for each Trust year representing the amount of such Participant's accounts that is not fully vested shall be used to reduce the employer's current and/or subsequent year's contributions under this Plan.

   However, under the limitations of Section 415 of the Internal Revenue Code (effective for Plan Years beginning after August 31, 1976), the total allocation of Employer Contributions and Forfeitures to any Participant may not exceed the lesser of 25 percent of compensation or $25,000 for any Plan Year.

How Is My Share of Investments Determined? As Company stock is contributed or paid for by the ESOP, a portion will be computed by the allocation formula described above and allocated to your Company Stock Account.

If the cash or other property contributed to the ESOP is not used to purchase Company stock, it may be used to purchase other investments, which will be allocated to Other Investments Accounts in the same way.

The Trust is authorized to purchase life insurance on "key-man" employees and also for the purpose of funding buy/sell agreements with Company shareholders. The Trust will be the owner, beneficiary, and premium payor of the life insurance policies pertaining to the ESOP. In the event that these provisions are utilized, special allocation procedures apply to the payment of premiums and the receipt of insurance proceeds on any such policy held by the Trust. A full explanation of the special allocation procedures will be provided to each Participant prior to making any such investment.

How Will I Be Advised of My Ownership Interest in the ESOP? Accounts will be maintained to record your interest in Company stock and other investments under the ESOP. Once each year you will be given a report that shows:

1. The balance of your accounts as of the preceding Anniversary Date.
2. The amount of Company Contributions allocated to your accounts.
3. The adjustment to your accounts to reflect your pro rata share of the income (or loss) of the ESOP for the year.
4. The new balances in each of your accounts, including the number of shares in your Company stock accounts. However, no stock certificates are made out in your name until shares are distributed to you after your employment terminates.

What Will Affect the Values of My Accounts? The following factors may affect the value of your accounts:

1. Employer contributions. Your accounts are credited with a portion of your Company's contribution based on formulas described above.
2. Income of the ESOP. The ESOP may receive dividends on Company stock and interest on other investments. Your share of the income is based on the relationship of your account balances to the total account balances of all Participants.
3. Change in value of ESOP assets. The current value of Company stock held by the ESOP is reflected by the earnings and asset value of the Company. The price of the stock will change each year depending largely on the earnings of your Company.

What Are My Distribution Rights under the ESOP? A Participant's Plan benefit will be computed as soon as possible after the close of the Plan Year in which his employment is terminated. The

Committee, after considering the wishes of you or your Beneficiary, will direct the Trustee to distribute your Plan benefit in accordance with one or more of the following ways or a combination of them:

1. In a lump sum or single payment.
2. In substantially equal annual, quarterly, or monthly installments plus accrued net income (or minus net loss). The amount of each installment may be based on a fixed number of years of payout or a fixed percentage of your Plan benefit. However, the period of installments may not exceed your life expectancy, or the joint life expectancy of you and your spouse (i.e., the average of your life expectancies).

In any event, unless you otherwise elect, the payment of benefits to you will begin not later than the sixtieth day after the close of the Plan Year in which the latest of the following events occurs:

1. You attain the Normal Retirement Date (age sixty-five).
2. You reach the tenth anniversary of the year in which you commenced participation in the Plan.
3. You terminate your services with the Employer.

What Will Be the Form of My Distribution? Distribution of Plan Benefits will be made entirely in whole shares of Company stock. Any amount remaining in your accounts that is insufficient to purchase a whole share of Company stock shall be distributed to you in cash.

What Is My Vested Share? Your vested share is the percentage of your account balances that you are entitled to have distributed when your service terminates. This vested share is your *ownership* share of your accounts.

The vesting of ownership benefits in employee accounts is structured to reward most those employees who, in the spirit of true owners, continue to contribute to the Company's success through the years.

When Do I Have Ownership of My Account?
1. Full ownership of your account. Your vested share will be 100 percent under the following circumstances:
   a. If you retire at or after the normal retirement age (age sixty-five). (Your participation and service may con-

tinue beyond your normal retirement date only upon request of the Company, or at your request with Company approval.)

b. If you die or become permanently disabled to work as a full-time employee.

c. If you have completed five full years of service with the Company.

2. Partial interest in your account.

a. If your participation in the ESOP ceases for any reason other than death, Disability, or normal retirement, the vested share of your account will depend on your number of full years of service with the Company, as shown in table 10.1.

TABLE 10.1. VESTING SCHEDULE

Full Years of Service at Date of Termination	Percent of Your Accounts Vested in You
Less than 1 year	0
1 Year	20
2 Years	40
3 Years	60
4 Years	80
5 Years	100

After Distribution, Will I Own My Shares without Restriction? Your shares will be your absolute private property as long as you wish to keep them. If you wish to dispose of your shares, however, they may be subject to a "right of first refusal." If so restricted, this means that the shares must be offered for sale first to the ESOP and then to the Company at the price that a prospective buyer is willing to pay. The ESOP and the Company each have thirty days (or together a total of sixty days) to accept the offer.

Is There a Market for My Company Stock? At the time of distribution of your shares, the ESOP or the Company may offer you a "put" option. The "put" option will give you the right, for a period of time not to exceed sixty days, to sell your stock to the ESOP or the Company at the fair market value as of the selling date, as established by the ESOP Committee in accordance with rules of the Internal Revenue Service. If the stock price moves up during that period, the "put" would increase your selling price.

Who Will Vote the Shares of Company Stock? Once the shares are distributed to you, you will have the power to vote them as long as you hold them. While held by the ESOP, the shares of Company stock will be voted at the direction of the ESOP Committee.

Can I Designate a Beneficiary? Yes. Shortly after you become eligible to participate in the ESOP, you will receive a form to be filled out to designate a Beneficiary in case of death.

May I Assign or Transfer My Account? No, your interest in the ESOP cannot be sold, assigned, or transferred prior to distribution to you. Furthermore, prior to distribution, your interest is not subject to any debts or claims against you except indebtedness to the Company.

May I Borrow from My Account? Yes. After your ESOP accounts are fully vested, you may apply to the Committee for a loan of any amount up to 50 percent of your vested share of your account balances as then estimated by the Committee. The Committee will make loans on a discretionary basis, but in a uniform and nondiscriminatory manner. All such loans will be treated as a Trust investment and will be repaid with interest. Each loan recipient shall receive a clear statement of the terms and charges, including the dollar amount and the annual interest rate of the finance charge.

How the ESOP Is Administered

Who Supervises the ESOP? The ESOP will be administered by a Committee composed of three individuals appointed by the Board of Directors of ESOT Average, Inc. The Committee will make such rules, regulations, computations, interpretations, and decisions and shall maintain such records and accounts as may be necessary to administer the ESOP.

Who Holds the Assets of the ESOP? A Trust has been established, pursuant to the ESOP, to hold the ESOP assets. It is a separate legal body with a trustee holding its assets for the exclusive benefit of all the Participants in the ESOP, pursuant to the terms of a Trust Agreement. The Trustee is Mr. Above Average of ESOT Average, Inc., 123 Any Street, Portland, Oregon 97204.

How Does the Trustee Know What to Do? The Trustee gets his instructions from the Trust Agreement itself and from the Committee. The Committee members are:

(one member of the management team)

(representative of the production department)

(representative of the rank and file membership)

all of ESOT Average, Inc., 123 Any Street, Portland, Oregon 97204.

These persons are also designated agents of the ESOP for the service of legal process.

How Are Questions and Claims Regarding Eligibility and Benefits Handled? All questions and claims regarding eligibility for participation and benefits under the ESOP should be directed in writing to the ESOP Committee. The Committee will provide written notice to any Participant or Beneficiary whose claim for benefits has been denied, setting forth the specific reason for the denial. Any denial of benefits may be appealed to the ESOP Committee and, upon written request, an opportunity for a hearing before the Committee will be granted.

Miscellaneous Information

1. The Company's Employer Identification Number (EIN) assigned by the Internal Revenue Service is 93-0000011 and the Plan (ESOP) number is 93-0000020.
2. The benefits provided by the ESOP are not eligible for the insurance provided by the Pension Benefit Guaranty Corporation.
3. The effective date of the ESOP is October 1, 1975. The Plan Year starts on October 1 and ends on September 30 (the Anniversary Date).

What Is the Future of the ESOP? It is the intention of the Company to continue the ESOP indefinitely, but it must of necessity reserve the right to alter or amend or even terminate the ESOP by action of the Board of Directors, in order to meet changing circumstances. It must be remembered, however, that in the event the ESOP should be terminated, all assets in the Trust must be used for the sole benefit of the Participants in the ESOP. *Nothing can revert to the company.*

How Can I Obtain More Information about the ESOP? The "Summary Plan Description" in this booklet is an accurate description of the Plan as of the date of printing the booklet. But please remember that this description does not take the place of the actual Plan and Trust documents, which govern at all times. *Copies of these documents, any amendments, and the annual report filed with the Department of Labor, may be inspected during regular business hours at our business office, 123 Any Street, Portland, Oregon 97204.* Also, for the cost of reproduction, copies of these ESOP documents, any amendments, and the Annual Report filed with the Department of Labor will be sent to you upon written request. If you should have any questions, please contact the Committee.

Tax Aspects of the ESOP

The principal federal income and estate tax consequences of participation in the ESOP under present provisions of the Internal Revenue Code are as follows:

Company Contributions Company Contributions to the ESOP that are allocated to your account are not taxable to you when made or credited.

Dividend and Other Income Dividends and other income on the assets held by the ESOP are not taxable to you when received by the ESOP or when credited to your accounts.

Distribution of Accounts on Termination of Employment

  I. Lump Sum Distributions. If your entire account under the ESOP is distributed within one year (i.e., in a "lump sum distribution") because of your retirement, total disability, death, or other termination of employment, you (or your Beneficiary) are taxable on—
   A. the amount of the original cost of the Company stock to the ESOP (or its fair market value when distributed, if that value is less than the original cost), *plus—*
   B. the amount of any cash plus the fair market value of any other property distributed from your Other Investments Account.

The taxable amount is ordinary income, but it may be eligible for a special ten-year averaging method under Section 402(e) of the Internal Revenue Code. This special method is available only for a lump sum distribution after death or if you have participated in the Plan for at least five years prior to the year of distribution. An election for special ten-year averaging may be made by filing IRS Form 4972 with your income tax return.

No tax is payable at the time of a lump sum distribution on any appreciation in the value of the shares while they were held by the ESOP. (The appreciation *is* taxed if you sell the shares later. See below.)

II. Installment Distributions. Unlike lump sum distributions, installment distributions attributable to Company Contributions are taxable entirely as ordinary income when received, at the fair market value. In the event of your death after termination of employment, any balance of installments due will be made to (and will be taxable to) your Beneficiary. Special tax rules under Section 72 of the Internal Revenue Code apply to installment distributions.

III. Special Death Benefits. In the event of death, a distribution (installment or lump sum) to your Beneficiary (or estate) may qualify for the special $5,000 income tax exclusion provided in Section 101(b) of the Internal Revenue Code.

Distribution During Employment

I. Dividends. If you receive a distribution of dividends on Company stock held by the ESOP, the full amount is taxable as ordinary income.

II. Partial Distributions. If you receive partial distributions of Company stock while you are employed, the full fair market value of the shares distributed is taxable as ordinary income.

Subsequent Sale of Stock. If you (or your Beneficiary) sell shares received from the ESOP, the sale will be taxed as a capital gain (or loss). The tax basis for determining capital gain (or loss) is the taxable amount at the time of distribution of shares as determined above.

You (or your Beneficiary) will realize long-term capital gain (or loss) on the sale of shares after distribution, if the shares have been held for over twelve months. If held for under twelve months, the shares when sold will produce a short-term capital gain (or loss). Also, if there has been a qualifying lump sum distribution upon termination of employment, and you later sell the shares, the portion of the gain represented by the appreciation in value while the shares were held by the ESOP will be taxed as long-term capital gain, regardless of whether the shares have been held for twelve months after distribution.

Stock Not Sold. If you hold the distributed shares until death, the tax basis for determining gain or loss on the subsequent sale of those shares by your estate or Beneficiary is the market value at the time of death. In other words, any appreciation existing at the time of distribution of the shares and also any further appreciation to the date of death will not be subject to income tax to your Beneficiary when the shares are sold.

Estate Tax Exclusion on Distributions after Death. If, on your death, a distribution is made by the ESOP to your Beneficiary (other than your estate), the amount of the distribution is excluded from your estate for federal estate tax purposes.

How Should a Participant Plan His Distribution? You should consult a qualified tax accountant or lawyer for individual tax advice before indicating a preference as to the mode of distribution and in determining the tax consequences of a distribution to you. This booklet is no substitute for legal advice.

PART II

MANAGEMENT TECHNIQUES FOR PROFIT PLANNING

11

RISK-MANAGEMENT TECHNIQUES IMPROVE PROFIT PLANNING

Webster's Third New International Dictionary of the English Language defines risk as "the possibility of loss, injury, disadvantage or destruction." One key to an improved profit center is departmental risk management studies. Most people want their companies to succeed, and companies best achieve their goals when employees develop their maximum potential. Studies have proven that employees are willing and able to cope with new ideas that are meaningfully structured toward job fulfillment. Those assigned the task of designing and charting risk-study manuals will achieve most by knocking at the human heart—not pushing. Therefore, my purpose in writing this chapter is to expose management-level personnel to the arts of conservation and retention of assets via the organization and implementation of risk-management strategy.

Too often today, businessmen and company executives overlook the profit-leveraging benefits that can result from eliminating or controlling losses. Shortsighted management often fails to recognize or investigate risks related to—

1. product selection and design;
2. use of a standard cost system vs. cost-control accounting;
3. potential marketing range;
4. long- and short-term financial requirements—i.e., lines of credit, assumption ratios relating to quantitative analysis,

insurance premiums vs. self-insurance, and other pertinent balance sheet components.

Success for the executive assigned to organize and implement risk-management principles is not likely to come unless he first employs three most needed ingredients: work! work! and work! Most of his associates will be preoccupied with such everyday business problems as customer demands, cash flow, competition, putting on new product lines or services, employee restlessness and work problems, production-scheduling demands, and last but not least, that never-to-be-forgotten measuring device we all use, ROI. Those drafting risk policies must therefore stand porter at their mental door and defend themselves against the no-change-wanted, don't-rock-the-boat forces. Expect them—they surely will come.

WHAT IS MEANT BY RISK MANAGEMENT?

Fundamentally, if a company is already using management studies to identify present and future uncertainties, cope with various alternatives, and analyze customer demands, production cost and price factors relating to elastic and inelastic demand and competition response, it is practicing the art of risk management.

Conventional investment studies follow the pattern of dilution decision making shown in figure 11.1.

Figure 11.1 illustrates how corporate executive planning generally starts with the executive decision makers. Upon accepting the plan, the CEO or executive in charge of flowing the design

FIG. 11.1.   CONVENTIONAL DILUTION DECISION PATTERN

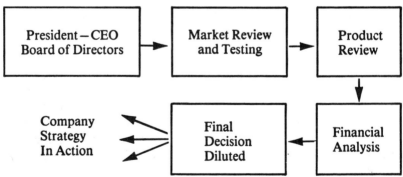

assigns the project study to (1) Marketing, (2) Product Study, and (3) Financial Analysis. The plan finally is rejected or placed into action upon approval by the vice-president in charge of finance. This linear process fails to utilize interaction feedback to deal with alternatives and uncertainties. Risk management interaction decision making would follow the pattern shown in figure 11.2.

FIG. 11.2. INTERACTION MANAGEMENT
DECISION PATTERN

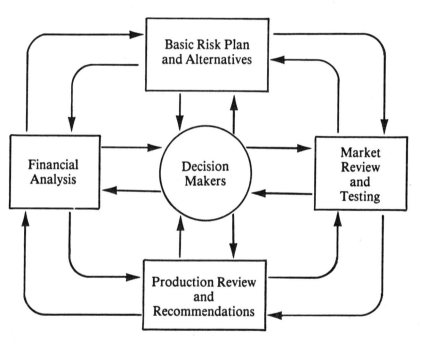

CEOs and decision-making boards of directors need to examine basic planning from various perspectives. The interaction management decision pattern shown in figure 11.2 illustrates how feedback of alternatives may be integrated in the project analysis, avoiding dilution. The interaction feedback process flowing through all pertinent departments produces alternatives and measurable risk factors, *intensifying rather than diluting* management awareness.

HOW TO IDENTIFY UNINSURABLE UNCERTAINTIES

Loss of market location or potential caused by service failures—such as out-of-stock conditions, late deliveries, ineffective inventory net sale controls, product obsolescence, or competitive encroachment—demand foresight of profit-motivated executives. Uninsurable risks generally pertain to market, production, finance, and politics. The following illustrates how each component is subject to loss of property or uncertainty exposure:

Marketing Risks

1. Competition's improved product or promotional campaign.
2. Price changes due to inelastic or elastic demands.
3. Customer likes/dislikes.
4. Fashion and style changes, local and foreign.

Production Risks

1. Production failures due to machinery.
2. Employee turnover, strikes.
3. Inability to obtain raw materials.
4. Inability to produce economically, solve production problems, or communicate effectively

Financial Risks

1. Capital solidus debt ratios.
2. Plant and equipment investments, cost of financing.
3. Quantitative analysis interaction, long-range planning.
4. Seasonal trends affecting working capital, cash flow.

Political Risks

1. Government intervention or control, or war.
2. National and international currency problems.
3. Free trade restrictions and/or harassment techniques.
4. Unreasonable taxation.

The corporate executive in charge of reviewing all departments of the company's operation regarding conservation and maintenance of profit—i.e., planning properly to protect company profits, that they may not be destroyed by some occurrence or condition that is outside the direct operation of the company—confronts risk problems such as the following.

Example

The risk executive's CEO informs him that a merger is being contemplated in order to secure a material supplier to protect against a possible future shortage problem. The cash required to transact the merger would be $1.5 million. What financial position is necessary to assure the company that future cash flow will not be jeopardized by this acquisition? What steps should be taken to assure the company of a future bank line of credit in case of economic reversals?

Possible Solutions

1. Have risk executive prepare quantitative analysis relating to cash-flow requirement for period affected by drain on cash.
2. Have vice-president in charge of finance negotiate a bank line of credit with a letter of intent covering the $1.5 million cash via amortization schedule, long-term arrangements.
3. Investigate such production alternatives as utilizing other material suppliers and creating a new product line not needing this particular material.
4. Have basic plan and all alternatives examined through the company's interaction decision program in order to weigh uncertainties affecting production, marketing, and finance.

PROCEDURES FOR COPING WITH RISK

Uncertainty problems allow management four alternatives: (1) assume the risk, (2) employ loss-prevention strategy, (3) transfer or shift the risk to others, (4) merge with others via probability analysis to measure the risk and/or minimize the losses (insure part of it, if possible).

Uncharted or improperly organized production-distribution sequences, coupled with the manufacturer's failure to employ interaction management decision making, causes consumer complaints and losses on sales and often causes the distributor to delist company products. Loss of profits due to failing to maintain proper in-stock service levels is a risk that should be controlled and guarded against. Companies generally measure service levels in terms of percentage of product available (it is not economically profitable to maintain 100-percent levels; therefore, quantitative studies are needed to determine the position that optimizes the ratio of production cost to profit). The risk study involves first establishing, via computer data input, a determination of where loss will likely occur first; second, performing a probability analysis concerning service-level failure; and third, formalizing the most profitable position into an organizational policy.

Data processing centers designed to analyze quantitative risk can feed in general information about production, marketing, probability of occurrence, and customer ordering policies. From these data, distribution costs of various levels can be ascertained. Measuring optimal service levels continually with fair ROI policies keeps the alert company in business and simultaneously affords workable solutions to customer response and needs. Following is a procedural technique that outlines the feasibility study that should precede risk management interaction planning.

1. Design and form a management team staffed with decision-making executives—i.e., those responsible for company strategy and profit goals. Prepare written instructions that clearly define procedural techniques, encourage competition and differentiation role playing, and allow technological freedom in order to encourage challenging and/or reexamining risk uncertainties.

2. Assignments should be submitted to the interaction management planning group in written form only. They should be given a cursory examination by the CEO and/or board of directors to determine their timeliness and profitability, then upon approval be assigned to the management team for control responsibility and policy decisions. A sample sequence of procedures by the management team follows.

   a. First forecast cash-flow requirements via payback-analysis accounting. Compare equity to debt procurement of funds as they relate to the discounted dollar.

   b. Set up budgetary controls to determine projected probabilities regarding cash applied and cash spent. Prepare pro forma financial statements that tie in to annual balance sheet projections.

c. Request each department executive to submit break-even charts and service-level matrix illustrations concerning risk problems.

d. Research and test consumer or buyer likes and dislikes (this is the foundation rationale of successful marketing). Establish a production policy concerning availability of resources, analyze public acceptance levels, and determine personnel availability as it relates to manufacturing and distribution requirements.

Risk management planning deals with communicating openly in order to measure and evaluate probabilities. The occurrence of a risk or uncertainty, whether the potential loss be small or large, should be studied, and the advantages and disadvantages weighed to determine a course of action. Corporate failures today are on the rise due to lack of concern for the management of nonspeculative risks that companies cannot escape. Economical elimination or reduction of risk problems, via management team studies, affords management peace of mind—meanwhile generating fresh ideas through interaction between profit-making departments.

12

EXECUTIVE POWER—

ITS USE

AND ABUSE

Too often, corporate management revolves in the vicious circle of use and abuse of executive power, consequently making only slight financial and behavioral progress. The established custom of giving management undisputed possession of the power to direct, alter, or eliminate projects and employees will be discussed and shown to be a major factor in corporate success or failure. Risk management is not generally considered in terms of the behavioral sciences; however, alert companies include nonspeculative risk factors in their considerations.

Pure power, void of emotion or inhibition, can compel obedience—it cannot stimulate subordinates to commit themselves to the organization. And the Machiavellian approach to gaining and keeping power, so generally thought of as good management strategy, often drives the company squarely into the endangered species category largely due to employee discontent, apathy, or turnover. However, Alexander Borgia, centuries ago, used Machiavellian power in an interesting way:

> The expedition of the French into Italy came with chalk in hand to mark up their lodgings, not with weapons [executive power] to force their passage.[1]

Similarly, executives effective in directing subordinates make their way quietly into those minds that are fit for it and of committed purpose.

---

1. *Francis Bacon,* Great Books of the Western World, vol. 30.

Executive power is rapidly becoming an impracticable exercise in any case—losing territorial placements to government and state laws, regulation, and intervention, or to union organization demands. There is a growing lack of commitment on the part of company employees to respect and support the organization. Decision-making executives often judge employee problems incorrectly because of inadequate understanding in the following three areas.

1. Seeing only with the eyes. Seeing what one believes, like believing what one sees, is a misuse of power, because the judgment is merely surface skimming devoid of reasoning and investigation. Imagination too often takes the forefront in the executive's mind, and he makes conclusions on the basis of what he wants to see—not what he does see.

2. Hearing only with the ears. Gossip and general tongue wagging have entered the arena of job evaluation and performance measuring. To be useful and foster satisfactory standards, what is heard should be translated into writing, weighed in a scale of actuality versus gossip, then given an acid test to determine purpose, substance, and feasibility.

3. Speaking only with the lips. Outdated management techniques devoid of feedback concepts and of upward communication prevent employees from contributing ideas or letting off steam and also stifle the satisfying of other psychological needs. Communication is the vital link between management and employees; failure to use upward communication strategy causes executives to be unaware of employee needs. Misused power is the result.

EXECUTIVE PURPOSE IN THE CORPORATE STRUCTURE

Making money for its owners is the mission of the corporate entity. Because of the need to generate a fair return on investment for corporate shareholders, the Establishment (managing executives and boards of directors) unmistakably becomes owner interested, conversely opposing the employees' welfare. Where divisional structuring fuels the separation by giving employees and management different "territorial rights," the arrangement can encourage employees to oppose management, resulting in less production and lower profits. Such a situation is usually resolved in a noncommittal means-to-an-end job routine. The lack of true dedication and company loyalty brings with it financial, production, and organizational woes. The corporate executive therefore must learn to knock at the human heart—not push. The point at which an organization can make money *plus* make employees feel they are being permitted to satisfy their psychological needs is the corporate line of demarcation that separates use from misuse of executive power.

Decisions confronting corporations today deal with uncertainties involving organizational power as it pertains to conservation and retention of key personnel, maintaining optimum service levels for products and services, and the communication sciences. Enlisting the talents, ideas, and support of others to complete mutual goal setting serves in itself to eliminate unpleasant developments.

Realizing that most persons have a built-in generator that, if given a current of kindness, becomes self-perpetuating and useful, companies are learning when and how to apply this quick-charge strategy. Successful executives understand and demonstrate sufficient leadership qualities to provide commitment fuel for themselves from the efforts produced by those that follow. This management law in operation, however unseen—*attitude reflects attitude*—alerts the executive to ponder ways to motivate and create synergy in his followers who might otherwise adhere to idiomatic patterns.

LEADERSHIP QUALITIES REPLACE EXECUTIVE POWER

Executive managers in charge of corporate policy are recognizing that learning is a mainstream activity that helps employees shift the basis of their self-realization and accomplishments from executive power to leadership strategy. Through a diagnostic process of self-awareness, employees can uncover their hidden character flaws; to eliminate them and replace them with right traits necessitates a personal commitment to learning. Formal training programs that encourage development of self-sufficiency skills require that each participant commit himself to demonstrate that "a man's reach should exceed his grasp."[2]

Achievement of self-sufficiency is essential to the development of both males and females; therefore the learning process should establish ground rules that will provide equal rights and dignity to

---

2. Robert Browning, "Men and Women."

all employees. The rationale for adhering closely to sound behavioral science techniques is to mate correctly the corporate growth factor with return-on-investment ratios. These management techniques should be monitored regularly and systematically through upward communication planning.

When upward communication is taught and encouraged, management can provide the company a standard to measure balance between supervisor and supervised. Establishing a framework of guidelines for implementing a company-approved program that enlists the support of all employees improves top management and simultaneously affords lower organizational levels a vehicle to contribute ideas and voice their concerns. Table 12.1 illustrates the advantages, for both the company and the managing executives, of using leadership techniques rather than power:

TABLE 12.1. ADVANTAGES OF USING
LEADERSHIP TECHNIQUES

PROBLEM	SOLUTION
The executives are running this organization the same way the founders ran it thirty years ago, keeping everything to themselves. Why aren't we better informed?	Have available for company employees a workable feedback program—e.g., a special number to call regarding company operational policies. Write potential callers explaining goals and purpose. Consider printing a quarterly company newsletter to inform all employees of current company news. Results will provide management and employees a foundation on which to demonstrate "we care" state-of-the-arts.
Top management doesn't care about us. Top brass isn't sensitive to our needs.	Have executives and company employees regularly air their differences. Company democracy provides management and employees a way to satisfy psychological and social needs.

Table 12.1—*Continued*

PROBLEM	SOLUTION
We work and give total commitment to the company—for what? What about our future retirement?	Recommend that all suggestions regarding improvement to company operations—i.e., schemes to eliminate waste, save time, and make profits—be submitted directly to the CEO. Each employee suggestion should be followed through and answered with reasons for acceptance or rejection. If company has an ESOP, improvements will help retirement benefits.

CONCLUSION

Only by practicing the art of true leadership can the executive inspire his subordinates to produce favorable results. Only as the follower commits himself to support the company and its profit goals can the executive rest in the truth, "The reward for a job well done is to have done it."[3] Restoring badly needed balance between the executives in top management and those they supervise brings with it self-satisfaction and sincere commitment to support the company, and it results in fulfillment of the purpose of forming a corporation in the first place—to produce profits.

---

3. *Michel de Montaigne,* Great Books of the Western World, vol. 25.

PART III

MERGERS

13

MERGER PLANNING

FOR THE

CLOSELY HELD

CORPORATION

Financial and technological changes affecting the family-controlled corporations require the closely held companies to investigate management skills pertaining to organizational perpetuity. Certain corporate organizational strategies—if correctly planned, organized, and implemented—will assure the founder of a family-controlled business of the profitable continuity of his successful company after he retires.

Building a cooperative team effort and providing a well-rounded package of fringe benefits—i.e., bonus, pension, and profit-sharing plans—do not in themselves complete the picture. Too often, the owner-president learns too late how to deal with the real root problems of continuing his company—finance, organization, and control. An extraordinary amount of usable information is available to presidents and manager-owners in census data and other government publications and materials concerning perpetuity, control, and finance. Properly used, these sources can help point out ways and means to cope with direct and indirect organizational problems. Traditionally, those who through fact-finding procedures analyze their company for the purpose of innovative company planning—e.g., finding ways to perpetuate company profitability—gain a stronger understanding of the whys and how-comes of employees' responses to company orientation sessions. Experience teaches if executives and employees have an umbrella of workable organizational policies, they generate increased production and profits, meanwhile maintaining that necessary ingredient "company mindedness."

THOUGHTLESS MANAGEMENT PLANNING

The Egyptians thought they knew how to operate and structure their companies to maintain control and perpetuity. Their organizational charts sought to demonstrate such impossibilities as, "Since I've made it, it's all mine—and shall be mine forever." King Tutankhamen, the last pharaoh of royal blood of the Eighteenth Dynasty, who was noted for supporting Egyptian art, three thousand years ago charted and planned how he, too, would organize and take his treasures with him. His failure was discovered when British archaeologist Howard Carter, in the year 1922, uncovered the king's treasures, consisting of over five thousand items all arrayed in four small chambers. Tutankhamen's lack of success was largely due to not recognizing he was a mortal—and that all businesses inevitably outlast their founders.

Surprisingly, few closely held corporate owner-presidents understand the financial advantages of properly charting their organization to assure good management control. To successfully ensure the continuity of the family-owned business requires sound management planning, if for no other reason than to maintain unity of command (dilution inevitably takes place when the founder-owner dies). To identify successful methodology that will not only promote continuity but also increase profits and rewards, the forward-thinking owner-manager should investigate the services of reputable organizations identified with good management techniques. One of the many factors that are oftentimes not realistically programmed is the organizational format, including a working board of directors familiar with company policies. The practical working board enables the company to operate in team fashion, within guidelines set by the owner, thereby affording the company organizational charting, control, and direction.

ORGANIZATIONAL CHARTING

The corporate president who designs and drafts a functional organizational chart reassures his management team—i.e., officers, the board of directors, bankers, financial advisors, and stockholders—of the company's continuous profitability and its perpetuity. The chart should be "architecturally" designed, keeping in mind the importance of its being understandable, usable, and capable of being demonstrated. The industry's pluses and minuses that directly affect the company's operation should be taken into account, and there should be written instructions describing basic policy. All this information should be recorded in the company's operational manual.

The basic reason for writing instructions regarding basic policy is to transmit the owner's intent and purpose that make the company a success. The owner-manager should ask himself these questions:

1. Does the business depend entirely on the personal following and talents of the owner-manager?

2. Is profitable continuity of the family company a major concern?

3. Is the company financially strong enough to support a second level of management that can be organized and trained?

Problems of centralization of control—e.g., unity of command that oftentimes begins, remains, and ends with the founder—are greatly lessened by the selection and utilization of peer-level board members. The improved theory and business practices brought about by an active, alert board of directors help avoid unnecessary and unprofitable business transactions.

PLANNING FUTURE CONTROL

The astute owner-manager, in planning continuous control of his thriving company, finds that the correct use of management services buttressed by outside expertise will provide specialization to areas that too often go unattended. Very few corporation presidents are familiar with and knowledgeable about the total operational needs of their companies. Most presidents find themselves occupied with the everyday battle for growth in sales, adequate cash flow to maintain equilibrium with production and labor costs, and other functional decisions regarding keeping the company afloat. To remain current with such highly controversial matters as industrial-labor relations, personnel and employee benefits, and administration and planning requires input from persons knowledgeable and experienced in those fields.

To perpetuate the family-owned business, the owner-president must plan, organize, and then implement the design that will regulate and control the organization. The real question that the president should ask himself is, Am I interested in the continuation of the successful operation after my retirement or passing? Realizing from experience that transactions with peer-level people, including outside management teams, never really result in flawless understanding, the owner-president should program several alternatives capable of substitutional changes, if required.

CONSERVATION AND RETENTION OF ASSETS

Financial success can be properly planned and organized by utilizing the right concept of conservation and retention of corporate assets. Today's need is not necessarily increasing sales or acquiring a larger portion of the market—it's having an awareness of how to budget and control the before-tax dollar. Today's alert banker wisely investigates what is credited to retained earnings on the corporate balance sheet and generally makes lines of credit in accordance with debt/equity ratios. Providing the banker realistic analytical data relating to company projections assures him that the line of credit extended to the company is secure and reasonable. Surprisingly, many family-owned-company executives in charge of finance fail to practice the art of banker-owner communication, except in times of economic problems that require immediate short- or long-term financing. Cultivating the loan officer with periodically scheduled meetings—including semiannual reports of corporate policies and budget-to-actual-cash-spent and cash-applied schedules, plus meaningful three- or five-year corporate planning projections—will bring favorable results that heretofore may have been unobtainable.

EARNING THE BANKER'S RESPECT

Bankers base loan decisions largely upon the prospective borrower's audited and unaudited statements. The reason for submitting financial statements supported with detailed worksheets is to provide continuity to a bank line of credit. Earning the respect of the banker is necessary to build lasting ties that result in substantial financial assistance in time of need. Keeping the banker knowledgeable of the company's organizational chart relating to perpetuity of management control cannot be stressed enough. The finance officer responsible for making loan decisions evaluates the company's projections regarding future sales and profitability in light of present and future organizational charts. Consequently, the alert owner-president tactfully communicates with the banker and keeps him informed of all aspects of his viable business.

VULNERABILITY TO CORPORATE TAKEOVER

Profitable family-owned companies are a target for takeover by a larger corporation. The smaller company today is likened to a rare antique—there are fewer of them every year. Readers of the nation's leading financial newspapers are becoming aware of the cash-laden corporations' desire to merge with or buy out closely owned companies. Merger activity increases in the bull market condition; conversely, when stock prices fall, the interest in mergers or acquisitions lessens.

The nontaxable merger for the purpose of business acquisition essentially follows one of these methods:

1. *Merger.* A stock-for-asset reorganization known as an "A" reorganization. Nonvoting common stock may be used in the transaction without losing the tax-free status of the exchange.

2. *Stock-for-stock exchange.* Referred to as a "B" reorganization. Only when 80 percent or more of the voting stock of the selling family-owned corporation is exchanged with the buyer's stock will a nontaxable situation result. This reorganization allows the purchasing corporation to continue under its own tax program.

3. *Stock-for-asset exchange.* A stock transaction commonly known as a "C" reorganization. It is similar to a merger; however, the consideration must be met solely with voting stock.

Merger-oriented planners aim at the family-owned business that has large cash accumulations. Generally they seek out companies whose balance sheets show minimal total assets (Federal Trade Commission ·records stated that during 1975 the mergers were small: 76 percent involved transactions of $1 million or less in assets). The steady reduction in the number of U.S. family-owned corporations, via taxable or nontaxable agreements, suggests that the alert company carefully investigate the following approach.

STRATEGY AND TECHNIQUES SHOULD A MERGER THREATEN

Generally, when the sellers structure the merger as a tax-free reorganization (where consideration to the sellers is all in stock of the acquiring corporation), the sellers will have no tax to pay. Should the sellers desire cash and other properties (a nonstock transaction), their proceeds become taxable. Structuring the merger becomes relatively simple when both parties agree as to what type of consideration will be acceptable. Before any real negotiation takes place, the following questions should be considered:

1. If the acquiring corporation's stock is leveraged to facilitate the merger, and it is overpriced due to a bull market, how will this overpricing affect the sellers?
2. What effect will stock dilution have on the acquiring corporation's earnings?
3. How will the trade-off amenities—e.g., marketability of the acquired stock, employment contracts, and other fringe benefits—relate to the seller's family tax planning?
4. What financial impact on the merger transaction will result from the 1976 Tax Reform Act (especially the elimination of the pre-1977 market value stepped-up basis)?

LEVERAGING PRICE EARNINGS AND ACCOUNTABILITY

Execution of the merger in order to maximize earnings per share (ROI) through preplanning the combining of interests (e.g., exchanging ownership interest in two or more corporations by exchange of securities) should strictly follow the opinions set out by the CPA Accounting Principles Board as outlined in volume 2 of its two-volume manual, pages 6639–6659.[4] The chapter entitled "Business Combinations,"—i.e., mergers—explains the correct conditions for pooling of interests, how to properly combine the

---

4. American Institute of Certified Public Accountants, New York, N.Y.

companies, and other pertinent accounting techniques. The accounting treatment for a combination merger of two or more corporations may significantly affect the financial condition and earnings of the merger for prior, current, and future periods. The same volume contains Accounting Research Studies No. 5 and 10, "A Critical Study of Accounting for Business Combinations," and "Accounting for Good Will," by Messrs. Wyatt, Catlett and Olson, valuable reading material for buyer and seller. Only as unsound opinions are replaced by understanding—i.e., through resolving merger catalytic reactions—will harmony prevail during the preinterview sessions.

If voting common stock is issued in order to effectually establish a combined stock interest, the pooling-of-interest accounting method is generally favored. In a nonstock transfer where cash distributions or other assets are disbursed, the purchase accounting method is required. In this case, the acquiring corporation records its costs as assets less liabilities assumed.

IMPORTANCE OF STRUCTURING PROGRAMMATICALLY

The management survey, preferably prepared by outsiders, will identify invaluable premerger data by which both the seller's and buyer's positions can be properly ratiocinated. The purpose of the survey is to analyze prior and current earnings per share in relation to divisional dilution; to compare an asset merger and a stock-for-stock proposal in light of the seller's and buyer's financial positions; and finally, to identify the methodology that will maximize the benefit to both parties in the merger. The investigative strategy shown in figure 13.1, if conscientiously and competently executed, will often bring to the surface problems that permit the merging parties to equate and define the transaction.

Valuation and Stock Strategy

The first stage shown in the figure—Valuation and Stock Strategy—is conceptually hard to determine but nevertheless most important and needful.

Before the valuation of the seller's corporation can be established, prior operating profits, including cash-flow projections, should be reviewed and evaluated. Extraordinary and nonrecurring expenses found in a company's profit-and-loss statement should be examined to determine their prior, present, and future role in

FIG. 13.1.   MERGER DEVELOPMENT TECHNIQUES

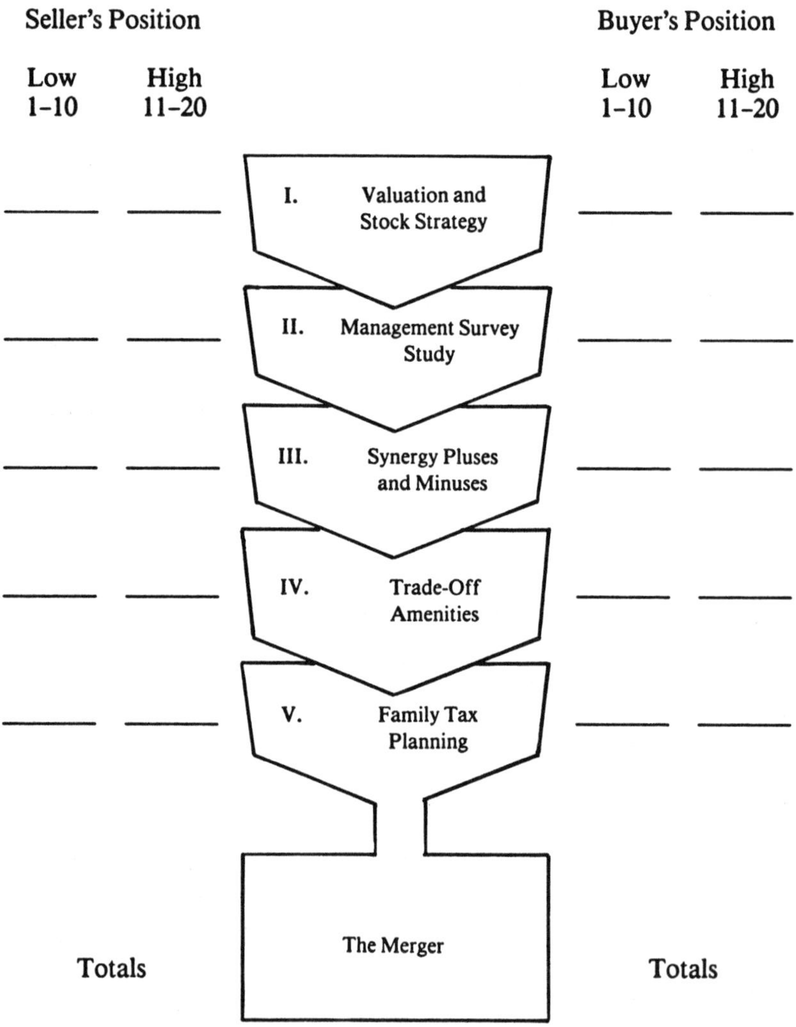

Seller's Position   Buyer's Position

Low	High
1–10	11–20

Low	High
1–10	11–20

I.   Valuation and
     Stock Strategy

II. Management Survey
     Study

III. Synergy Pluses
     and Minuses

IV. Trade-Off
     Amenities

V.   Family Tax
     Planning

The Merger

Totals   Totals profit factors and/or cash-flow performances of a merged entity. If items on the list below are found, they should be thoroughly researched to determine whether or not they are of the ordinary and necessary category.

1. Depreciation write-offs of capitalized items vs. direct write-offs
2. Bad debt write-off policies, including inventory accountability
3. Excessive administrative expenses pertaining to advertising, payroll, rents, and general operating costs
4. Travel and entertainment expenses

The valuation method, including stock strategy, properly designed and organized, affords the purchaser and seller reasonable assurance that the transaction can pay its own way within an accountable time period. This study generally determines the low or high dollar placement value pertinent to the seller's and buyer's positions.

Management Survey Study

The management survey should concentrate on the advantages and disadvantages of purchasing the assets through a total stock purchase or a stock-for-stock merger. Questions of favorable or unfavorable income tax position generally center around properties covered by Sections 1245 and 1250 of the Internal Revenue Code. The premerger management survey should have as its central theme whether merger proceeds will qualify for ordinary income or capital gains tax treatment. The survey results should include brief pertinent data on the following items:

1. The nature of the business and the history of the enterprise from its inception
2. The economic outlook in general and the condition and outlook of the specific industry in particular
3. The book value of the stock and the financial condition of the company
4. The earning capacity of the company, including its dividend-paying capacity

5. Whether or not the company has goodwill or other intangible value

6. The market price of stocks of corporations engaged in the same or a similar line of business having their stock actively traded in a free and open market, either on an exchange or over the counter

The synergistic potential of the merger should be evaluated with special attention to management, financing, marketing, and production. Enough similarity in outlook and approach must exist to enable buyer and seller to work together. Merger failures are often caused by mismatch of size, by the inability of the acquired company to follow the acquirer's reasoning, and by poor reporting relationships that affect lines of communication between the two companies. The exercise will lead to conclusions regarding strategic planning, including basic planning to maximize organization effectiveness.

Trade-off amenities, including family tax planning, usually take center stage action when cash flow and estate programming are considered. For instance, the study should deal with key questions regarding objectives. Further decisions will be based on these objectives; so they should be established before undertaking other important steps in negotiations. The purchaser should realize the necessity of proper internal evaluation of his own resources as they pertain to (1) granting the seller's present and future benefits— e.g., consulting fees and/or employment contracts; (2) definable reporting procedures that will regulate the acquired company; and (3) plans and controls that spell out the way management will perform immediately after the takeover. Simultaneously, family tax planning will come into play as the trade-off amenities become clear and acceptable to both parties. Only through in-depth review of each case as it relates to estate planning, particularly as applicable under the 1976 Tax Reform Act, can the financial arts of conservation and retention be applied.

Estate consultants that specialize in family tax planning would be most valuable in contributing ideas as to (1) how the ownership of the stock should be programmed, (2) the present and future use of a trust as it pertains to control and dollar usage, and (3) sound gift and estate-planning procedures.

The most popular kinds of tax-free mergers are asset mergers and stock-for-stock mergers. A typical tax-free asset merger involves the transfer to the buyer of the selling corporation's assets (subjecting the buying corporation to the seller's liabilities), and the simultaneous distribution of the buying corporation's stock to the stockholders of the selling corporation—who then turn over their stock in the seller. The stock-for-stock tax-free transaction requires a stockholder of the selling corporation to exchange his stock for stock of the buying corporation, without an involvement of asset transfer accounting. Figure 13.2 shows consequences to the buying and selling corporations of transfers and of a "B" reorganization exchanging stock-for-stock.

The two basic classifications (each useful for different purposes) require the designers to use extreme caution when "boot," either cash or other property, is offered as part of the consideration.

What, then, are the high and low percentage positions that the buyer and seller will find in the potential merger arrangement? The merger development technique shown in figure 13.1, closely studied and evaluated, requires the merger strategist to adhere to the following procedures.

1. Design and organize the merger plan, which shall include specifics regarding communications between the selling company and the purchasing company prior to and after the takeover.

2. Establish ground rules relating to employees to be severed, vacation policies, and pension/profit-sharing provisions.

3. Consider accounting, legal, and financial policies that will materially affect the buyer and the seller.

4. Request written documents to substantiate how the prospective purchaser intends to merge the selling corporation into the parent corporation.

5. Analyze performance of buyer and seller as it relates to past, present, and future abilities in marketing, sales, productivity, and ROI.

These merger techniques are useful to both the willing seller and the willing buyer. As opposed to the "nine-iron theory" of corporate takeover, the premerger techniques provide the willing buyer and seller with a unique approach to evaluating their pro-

FIG. 13.2.   CONSEQUENCES TO BUYER AND SELLER
OF ASSET-TRANSFER
AND STOCK-FOR-STOCK MERGERS

"A" OR "C" ASSET TRANSFER REORGANIZATION

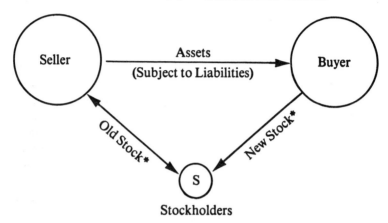

*The buyer's new stock is issued to stockholders of selling corporation upon their surrender of stock in seller and the transfer of assets from seller to buyer.

"B" STOCK-FOR-STOCK REORGANIZATION

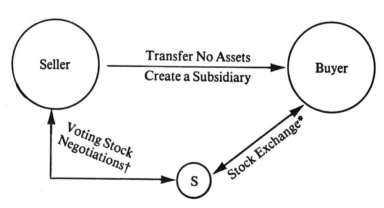

Stockholders of Selling Corporation

*Seller surrenders stock upon receiving buyer's voting stock.

†The stockholders of selling company must through minutes/documents agree with the selling corporation to transact over 80 percent of their voting stock *prior to exchange of stock with buyer.*

spective benefits. All relevant facts and figures must be reviewed and studied before the buyer or seller makes the formal decision to merge. Gathering essential data in order to weigh the pros and cons of a pending merger transaction enables the financial entrepreneur to determine objectives and measure the feasibility of the merger transaction.

GENERAL OVERVIEW AND CONCLUSION

A positive approach to sound management principles will result from gaining a balanced perspective concerning the family-owned corporation's management tools—e.g., organizational charting to provide perpetuity, leveraging assets via tax-deductible programming, and designing workable controls. The closely held business can be perpetuated only as the corporation understands the practicality of organizing and implementing financial data; of establishing a workable plan; of structuring correctly, then controlling.

That endangered species, the family-owned corporation, must come to the realization that its primary responsibility does not rest with daily operational procedures. Every effort should be made to chart the closely held company toward "endless-duration planning," i.e., providing organizational controls and perpetuity to family tax planning. Managerial autonomy—attained partly by having key executives participate in company stock ownership—will do much to provide a workable plan. The owner-president should consider cash needs and the high costs of administration and estate taxes, and measure these costs against his greatest asset —the continuity of the family-owned business.

PART IV

ESTATE

PLANNING

14

ESTATE AND GIFT

TAX PLANNING

FOR THE

COMPANY EXECUTIVE

After twenty-four months of hearings, proposals, leveraging arguments, and finally reaching acceptable agreements, the Federal Tax Reform Act was given birth on October 4, 1976, when President Gerald Ford signed the Act into law. Most of the Act's provisions became effective on January 1, 1977, making major changes in our federal estate and gift tax laws for the first time in thirty years.

Under pre-1977 law, Congress was not as generous in providing middle-bracket estates ($100,000 to $500,000) the definable retention and conservation techniques that now, thanks to the House Ways and Means Committee's tax bill HR 14844, can be found scattered throughout the Act. The committee's gift and estate tax bill was mainly a response to the existing inequities in tax rates, the harsh treatment being afforded the $100,000-to-$500,000 estates, and other factors pertaining to excessive tax preferences.

UNIFICATION OF ESTATE AND GIFT TAX RATES

Before the unified rate schedule was introduced in 1977, the law allowed each donor a specific lifetime exemption from gift tax of $30,000 and permitted his estate to deduct $60,000 from the decedent's gross estate in computing the taxable estate. Previous gift tax calculations, which enjoyed a 25-percent dollar advantage over estate tax rates, have been replaced by an integrated formula—a

197

unified estate and gift tax credit of $30,000 in 1977, $34,000 in 1978, $38,000 in 1979, $42,500 in 1980, and $47,000 in 1981 and thereafter. Technical mathematical calculations confront executors of estates of those dying after 1976; however, in general, the five-year phase-in provides all estates an equivalent exemption ranging from $120,667 in 1977 to $175,625 in 1981 and later years. Thus, when the credit is fully phased in, the exemption will be $85,625 more than the pre-1977 total of $90,000, providing estate planners more leveraging and retention benefits. Table 14.1 shows how the new credit translates into exemption dollars.

TABLE 14.1.   UNIFIED TAX CREDIT
AND EXEMPTION EQUIVALENT

Death in the Year	Unified Tax Credit	Exemption Equivalent
1977	$30,000*	$120,667
1978	34,000	134,000
1979	38,000	147,333
1980	42,500	161,563
1981 and after	47,000	175,625

*For gifts during 1977, refer to Internal Revenue Code Sections 2010 and 2505 (added by 1976 Act—2001) re: "Transitional ruling for certain gifts made after 12-31-76 and prior to 1-1-78."

To learn what the unification of estate and gift tax rates means to the family tax planner, one must first research, then understand how the schedule applies to both lifetime gifts and testamentary (death) transfers made after December 31, 1976. This "new-old approach to collecting taxes" eliminates the dual rate structure for gift tax and estate tax. Simultaneously it washes out the previous bargaining techniques by which gifts were taxed at only three-quarters of corresponding estate tax rates (which afforded tax-payers a method of shifting property from the highest estate tax rate to the lower gift tax structure via lifetime gifting).

LEVERAGING THE CREDIT AND LIFETIME GIFTING

Under the new Tax Reform Act, each spouse receives a full unified credit, and in 1981 and after, the $47,000 tax credit affords each spouse an exemption equivalent of $175,625. Equalizational estate planning, i.e., organizing and designing the two estates to balance assets between spouses, allows each spouse to leave up to $175,625 *free of estate tax,* compared to $60,000 under the old law. Estate planners should take a hard look at equalizational programming concerning the $351,250 tax-free placement. The unification procedures increase the effective individual exemption, which ultimately enables a taxpayer dying in 1981 to leverage tax-free transfers totalling $525,000 *with no federal estate tax,* if he leaves his estate to his wife (through maximum use of lifetime gifts to spouse, including gifts of interest in joint tenancies).

Under the old law, gifts made within three years of death were included in the gross estate unless the estate proved they were not made in contemplation of death. Under the unification ruling, the executor is required to include all transfers (less the $3,000 annual exclusion described below) made within three years of death as part of the decedent's estate regardless of the state of health at the time of death, and in addition thereto, any gift tax paid is also added back into the gross estate and taxed.

The gift program is good news. Up to $3,000 per donee per year now passes tax free—void of any adverse impact on tax due at death—and the Act excludes the gift from the decedent's estate even though death was anticipated when the gift was made. Obviously, for any gift to be valid, the donor must be of sound mind at the time of the gifting. Employing gift-splitting strategy—i.e., making annual tax-free gifts to each donee of $3,000, or $6,000 for married couples—will remove ceiling assets from the donor's estate, resulting in lower settlement costs and estate taxes. Gift splitting is a unique way to generate "nontaxable gift exclusions" that cannot later be added back into the estate to create higher taxes or a higher tax bracket. The Act, for example, allows a parent who has three married children and eight grandchildren an escape route by which conservation of $42,000 per year may be realized with no transfer tax. (Donees are: three children, their three spouses, and eight grandchildren. Fourteen donees @ $3,000 each = $42,000.)

The new law provides an unlimited gift tax marital deduction for the first $100,000 in gifts to one's spouse during one's lifetime. And effective January 1, 1977, the Act increases the marital deduction ceiling for estates of under $500,000. The estate tax mari-

FIG. 14.1.   DIRECT VERSUS PLANNED DISTRIBUTION DESIGN

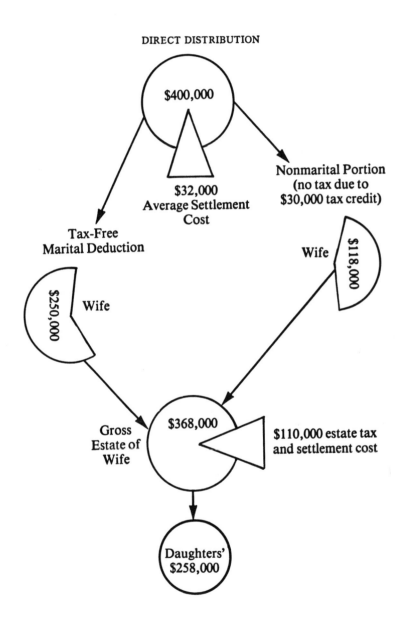

DIRECT DISTRIBUTION

Fig. 14.1.   Direct versus Planned
Distribution Design—*Continued*

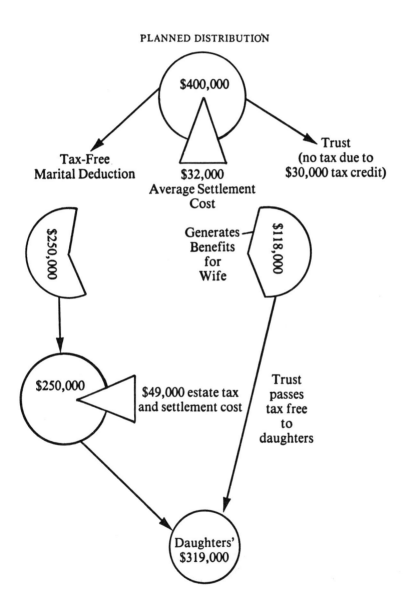

PLANNED DISTRIBUTION

tal deduction is $250,000 or 50 percent of the adjusted gross estate, whichever is greater. The gift tax marital deduction's first $100,000 lifetime gift to a spouse is completely free of tax; the second $100,000 gift has no deduction; but for gifts in excess of $200,000 there is a 50 percent deduction. Properly using the unlimited gift tax deduction, plus penciling out basic financial strategy for equalizing the spouses' estates, will generally result in lower administrative costs and lower taxes, meanwhile providing more cash flow. Planners should keep in mind that, starting January 1, 1977, husband and wife are each entitled to a full unified tax credit.

PLANNING CONSIDERATIONS AND TECHNIQUES

Due to the effect on the estate of the graduated rate tax structure, an organized and efficient placement of the marital deduction prior to the death of either spouse can save thousands of dollars including the reduction of administration and settlement costs. Additional conservation and retention of client investments may be achieved during the surviving spouse's lifetime by prudently investing the savings that are generated from the marital deduction. Results due to this modus operandi include more cash dollars for the surviving spouse to spend and, equally beneficial, more property conserved for succeeding generations.

Direct versus Planned Distribution

Example When Mr. Prosperous Citizen died in an automobile accident in 1977, he was survived by his wife and two daughters. During his working life, he had accumulated $400,000 in estate assets. Mrs. Citizen had no estate of her own. She had occupied her time raising the family and supporting her husband in his business. Mr. Citizen left a simple will leaving everything outright to his wife (direct distribution). Figure 14.1 compares the result with the outcome of planned distribution.

As shown in the figure, the 1976 Tax Reform Act enabled Mr. Prosperous Citizen to leave a $400,000 estate without owing any federal estate tax. The $250,000 marital deduction (or one half of any adjusted gross estate, whichever is greater), combined with leveraging the $30,000 1977 unified tax credit, enabled the parents to plan their distribution—ultimately leaving their daughters the $319,000.

Planned rather than direct distribution resulted in $61,000 additional dollars for the two daughters. Setting up a will allowing for separate placement of the portions of the estate covered and not covered by the marital deduction made possible this 15¼ percent cash-flow advantage.

The large dollar savings were brought about because the trust passed completely tax free, at the wife's death, to the two daughters. Had the trust assets appreciated due to the trustee's management skills, this increase in dollars also would have gone directly to the two daughters, completely tax free.

Important Document Insertions

Substantive clauses, even though restrictive in use, are often overlooked in treating the marital deduction. They include common disaster, simultaneous death, and fixed-period survivorship. The attorney selected to draft wills or trust agreements should have a workable knowledge of these "protective insertions," mainly to assure the client that, if they prove advantageous, they will be utilized in drafting the legal work. Consider the following.

I. The common disaster clause is generally written to permit the husband's relatives rather than the wife's to be the beneficiaries of his property if the wife dies from the same common disaster that killed the husband, but the wife lived for only a short period. Obviously, litigation might arise in the event that the final audit questions the time of death or the length of time the wife survived.

II. The simultaneous death clause permits the establishment of a provision that creates a presumption as to which spouse died first. In order for property to qualify for the marital deduction, the inheriting spouse must survive the decedent. The planner should also consider the following questions.

A. Does the plan include directives and alternatives concerning estate equilibrium?

B. What doubling up of direct and indirect fees will be incurred if the property flows through two estates?

C. How will total spendable dollars be affected by the Uniform Simultaneous Death Act (which presumes each spouse to have survived the other) should the estate result in no marital deduction?

III. The six-month survival clause relates to the interest of a spouse who survives for a limited period. A time clause has pluses and minuses that should be evaluated, especially if the period exceeds six months. For example, complications may result if death is caused by a common disaster, or if the surviving spouse suffers a lingering illness necessitating cash flow.

The 1976 Tax Act provides a fractional-interest rule that drastically changes the estate tax picture regarding joint tenancies, i.e., pertaining to ownership of property acquired by husband and wife after December 31, 1976. Under the new Act rules, one half of a qualified joint interest in property acquired by husband and wife after December 31, 1976, will be included in the decedent's gross estate regardless of which joint tenant furnished the consideration. To qualify as a joint interest, the following conditions must be met.

1. The interest must have been created by one or both of the joint tenants (an inheritance from a third party will not meet the requirement).

2. If the interest was created by one of the parties, who then gave joint tenancy participation to the other party, the second party's share will qualify as a joint interest only if the donor elected to treat the transfer as a taxable gift at the time of transfer (IRC Section 1250), "Real Property."

3. In the case of personal property, the creation of the joint interest must have been a completed gift as regulated by the gift tax rules.

4. The joint tenants must be limited to the two spouses—no third parties can have an interest in the tenancy.

Redesigning pre-1977 joint interests to qualify under the new fractional interest rule requires the planner to terminate the old pre-1977 tenancy, simultaneously creating a new joint tenancy. The new joint tenancy would be eligible for treatment as a taxable gift, thereby enabling the property to avoid the often undesirable "consideration furnished test." The unlimited gift tax marital deduction for the first $100,000 of lifetime gifting makes reorganizing the taxpayer's old joint tenancy ownership a unique approach to equalizing the spouses' estates.

Filing Gift Tax Returns for Estate Purposes

Gift tax returns for the years after 1976 must be filed on a quarterly reporting schedule only when the sum of (1) the taxable gifts made during the calendar quarter plus (2) all other taxable gifts made during the calendar year for which a return has not been filed exceeds $25,000.

If the U.S. Treasury makes an adjustment to a gift or estate tax return determining a higher valuation, the Internal Revenue Service must upon written request supply information on what method the treasury used to do so, under the provisions of the 1976 Tax Reform Act. Under the old law, the IRS was not compelled to disclose to an executor or donor the basis for making a higher valuation.

The 1976 Act changes the financial threshold necessitating the filing of an estate tax return, as shown in table 14.2.

TABLE 14.2. THRESHOLD FOR FILING
AN ESTATE TAX RETURN

Return Required for Decedent Dying in	Only if Gross Estate Exceeds
1977	$120,000
1978	134,000
1979	147,000
1980	161,000
1981 and after	175,000

Carryover basis for inherited property now replaces the old law that, prior to January 1, 1977, allowed the beneficiaries a stepped-up estate tax value for property acquired from a decedent. Property received from the decedent dying after December 31, 1976, carries with it the decedent's adjusted basis—i.e., its value immediately before his death, determined by a formula similar to the present method of valuing property for gift purposes. However, this basis is increased by the following four adjustments.

1. The carryover basis will be increased by the federal and estate tax paid by the estate brought about by the appreciation in the property.

2. Unrealized appreciation, regardless of the estate tax paid, affords each estate a minimum basis adjustment of $60,000.

3. When property acquired from a decedent requires the recipient to pay a state succession tax (attributable to appreciation), the imposed additional state tax will be allowed as an adjustment.

4. Under Code Section 1023 (h), "Adjustment," known as the "fresh start" provision, decedent's assets owned and inventoried as of December 31, 1976, are valued at their worth as of that date, as a basis for future capital gains treatment.

Obviously, all the ramifications of such complex and far-reaching legislation cannot be compressed into a few pages, but it is important that estate planners with responsibility for family tax planning be alerted to the certainties, restrictions, and benefits contained in the 1976 Tax Reform Act.

Appendix C comprises samples of forms for compiling data necessary for family estate planning.

APPENDIX A
SAMPLE MANAGEMENT
AUDIT

TABLE A.1. GENERAL CORPORATE INFORMATION

To properly prepare a MANAGEMENT AUDIT regarding the benefits your Company would derive from the organizing and implementation of an Employee Stock Ownership Trust, we will need financial information relating to the Company's operation. We agree that any material furnished by you will be reviewed in strict confidence and professionalism.

1. Company name: _____
   Address: _____
   Telephone number: _____
   Officer to contact
   regarding financial questions _____
2. Reasons to consider an ESOT as relating to your Company:
   _____ Provide a market for the sale of Company stock
   _____ Procure new financing using pretax dollars
   _____ Refinance present Corporate debt, using pretax dollars
   _____ Generate a market for the express purpose of purchasing a subsidiary
   _____ Distribute ownership of Company among employees in order to increase efficiency and lower operating cost
   _____ Generate cash flow to finance a tender offer for the repurchase of Corporate stock
3. General information regarding stock:
   Date incorporated: _____
   State in which Company resides: _____
   Authorized number of shares: _____
   Classes of stock authorized: _____

Major stockholders and shares held by each:

Table A.1—*Continued*

Stockholder Name	Shares Owned	Age	Title	Active/ Inactive

Dividend history:

Year	Amount Paid	Year	Amount Paid	Year	Amount Paid

4. Any buy/sell agreements in Company? _____ Yes _____ No
5. Last year's actual gross annual payroll: _____
   Salaried: $ _____   Hourly: $ _____
6. Accounting year of Company: _____
7. Estimated pretax income for current year: $ _____
8. Pretax income for prior three years:

Year	Pretax Earnings	Federal Tax Paid	State Tax Paid

9. Projected pretax earnings and payroll (covered) for next three
   years:

Year	Pretax Earnings	Covered Payroll

Table A.1—*Continued*

10. Please attach the three prior years' audited or unaudited financial statements of the Corporation.
11. Present profit-sharing plan:
Net trust equity: _____ Date determined: _____
Date plan installed: _____ Formula: _____
General accounting information, profit-sharing plan:

Year	Amount Contributed	Covered Payroll

12. Detail existing fringe benefits: _____
13. Pension plan information:
Date   Percent of
established: _____ payroll: _____
Stated benefits: _____
Assumed benefits: _____
Money purchase: _____
14. Employees under collective bargaining agreements, if any:
Number of union employees: _____
Union workers' annual payroll: $ _____
Number of nonunion employees: _____
Nonunion employees' annual payroll: $ _____
15. Please return this completed report to:

H. Griffin Ewing Consultants
Pioneer Park Building, P.O. Box 435
715 S.W. Morrison St.
Portland, Oregon 97207

TABLE A.2. CORPORATE FIVE-YEAR BALANCE SHEET

	1970	1971	1972	1973	1974
Current Assets					
Cash	$ 1,837,637	$ 2,064,409	$ 3,097,019	$ 3,660,459	$ 4,365,206
Current Installments on Lease Contracts	4,964,134	5,984,022	7,399,263	8,475,549	10,546,692
Accounts Receivable	858,492	453,260	630,626	1,144,733	997,245
Total Receivables	$ 5,822,626	$ 6,437,282	$ 8,029,889	$ 9,620,282	$11,543,937
Inventory	$ 1,140,231	$ 1,861,527	$ 3,083,028	$ 2,392,498	$ 3,080,861
Property for Sale	—	343,848	—	—	—
Prepaid Expenses	265,007	458,692	794,091	1,039,703	1,281,351
Total Current	$ 9,065,501	$11,165,758	$15,004,027	$16,712,924	$20,271,355
Noncurrent Contracts					
Lease Contracts	$14,322,635	$17,164,389	$21,179,032	$25,753,817	$29,914,134
Less Current Portion Other	76,093	141,650	32,561	139,557	186,262
Total Noncurrent Receivables	$14,398,728	$17,306,039	$21,211,593	$25,893,374	$30,100,396
Lease Contracts Receivable—					
Uninstalled Displays	3,876,131	6,829,125	7,776,456	9,861,814	9,937,507
Property and Plant	1,483,412	1,529,701	1,613,244	1,644,547	2,147,781
Deferred Charges and Other Assets	486,243	929,788	1,137,779	1,194,270	1,568,755
Total Assets	$29,310,015	$37,760,411	$46,743,099	$55,306,947	$64,025,794

Table A.2.—*Continued*

	1970	1971	1972	1973	1974
Current Liabilities					
Notes Payable to Bank	$ —	$ —	$ —	$ —	$ 1,300,000
Accounts Payable	596,369	569,668	1,077,582	1,297,270	1,719,659
Accrued Expenses	198,983	218,880	329,126	290,903	474,318
Current Taxes	703,784	788,920	943,809	1,138,212	1,423,493
Long-Term Debt	2,801,000	3,838,977	5,266,012	10,500	14,743
Other Debt	336,365	120,542	36,500	29,000	—
Total Current	$ 4,636,501	$ 5,536,987	$ 7,653,029	$ 2,765,885	$ 4,932,213
Deferred Credits—					
Estimated Cost to Install and Maintain	$ 2,114,581	$ 2,996,679	$ 4,213,232	$ 5,327,240	$ 4,566,088
Estimated Unearned Revenue	1,761,550	3,832,446	3,563,225	4,534,574	5,371,419
Total	$ 3,876,131	$ 6,829,125	$ 7,776,456	$ 9,861,814	$ 9,937,507
Unearned Maintenance	5,737,142	6,665,335	6,918,067	7,520,002	8,116,576
Deferred Taxes	2,009,005	2,429,418	2,745,828	3,458,768	4,027,134
Long-Term Debt—Bank	8,099,000	11,071,000	15,694,350	24,413,078	28,420,000
Long-Term Debt—Other	—	121,084	122,085	172,815	204,713
Stockholders' Equity					
Common Stock	909,000	909,000	909,000	909,000	909,000
Paid-in Capital	9,650	9,650	9,650	9,650	9,650
Retained Earnings	4,033,586	4,188,212	4,914,634	6,195,935	7,469,001
Total Equity	$ 4,952,236	$ 5,107,462	$ 5,833,284	$ 7,114,585	$ 8,387,651
Total Liabilities and Equity	$29,310,015	$37,760,411	$46,743,099	$55,306,947	$64,025,794

TABLE A.3. CORPORATION FIVE-YEAR PROFIT STATEMENT

	1970	1971	1972	1973	1974
Revenue on Displays					
Lease Sales	$ 8,925,743	$10,103,141	$13,820,175	$15,142,952	$18,154,485
Less Unearned Finance	1,291,220	1,250,107	1,587,658	1,609,709	2,488,561
Less Unearned Maintenance	2,075,774	2,208,340	1,944,326	2,045,849	2,188,264
Net Lease Sales	$ 5,558,749	$ 6,644,694	$10,388,191	$11,487,394	$13,477,660
Direct Sales	587,742	1,669,627	1,368,020	2,731,789	2,681,213
Net Revenue, Displays	6,146,491	8,314,321	11,756,211	14,219,183	16,158,873
Cost to Build, Displays	2,332,303	4,060,537	4,837,411	4,098,245	5,277,513
Gross Profit, Displays	3,814,188	4,253,784	6,918,800	9,120,938	10,881,360
Finance Revenue Earned	713,924	928,148	1,185,170	1,370,326	1,488,734
Maintenance Revenue Earned	1,459,194	1,856,365	1,908,704	2,080,015	2,452,407
Net Revenue, Installed Displays	$ 5,987,306	$ 7,038,297	$10,012,674	$12,571,279	$14,822,501
Operating Expenses					
Interest	839,593	1,018,435	1,122,526	1,454,770	2,635,930
Maintenance	1,894,520	1,436,383	2,080,422	2,278,181	2,972,827
Selling, Gen. & Adm.	2,878,165	3,792,858	5,459,023	5,704,710	6,910,022
Total Operating Exp.	$ 5,612,278	$ 6,247,676	$ 8,661,971	$10,188,119	$12,518,779
Operating Income	375,028	790,621	1,350,703	2,383,160	2,303,722
Other Income (deducts)	38,159	89,229	99,377	(4,260)	53,886
Earnings before Tax	336,869	701,392	1,450,080	2,378,900	2,357,608
Net Earnings	$ 198,736	$ 337,026	$ 907,622	$ 1,463,101	$ 1,500,316

FIG. A.1.   ACTUAL GROSS SALES, 1970–74

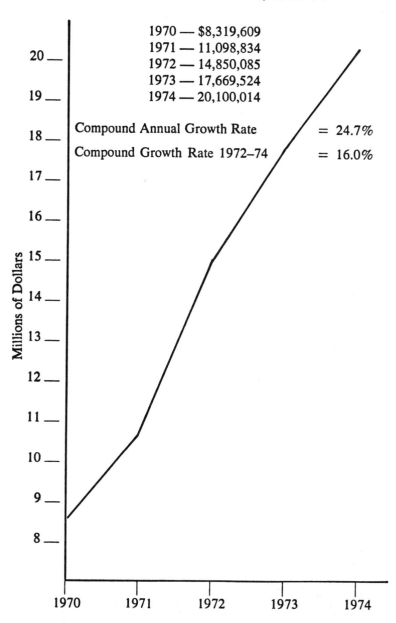

1970 — $8,319,609	
1971 — 11,098,834	
1972 — 14,850,085	
1973 — 17,669,524	
1974 — 20,100,014	
Compound Annual Growth Rate	= 24.7%
Compound Growth Rate 1972–74	= 16.0%

FIG. A.2. ACTUAL NET EARNINGS, 1970–74

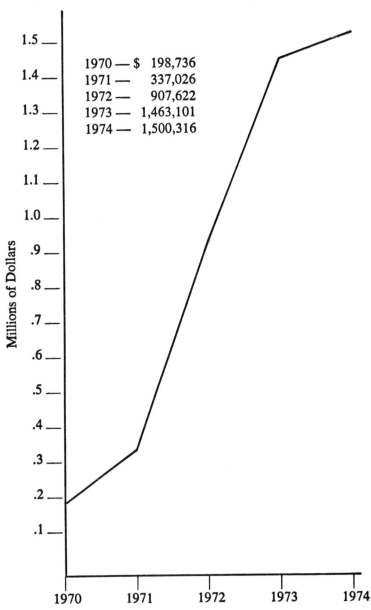

1970 — $ 198,736
1971 —   337,026
1972 —   907,622
1973 — 1,463,101
1974 — 1,500,316

FIG. A.3. PROJECTED GROSS SALES, 1975–79
(Based on 1970–74 compound annual growth rate of 24.7%)

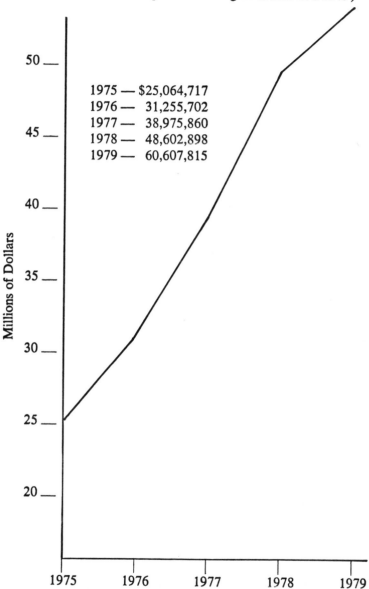

1975 — $25,064,717
1976 — 31,255,702
1977 — 38,975,860
1978 — 48,602,898
1979 — 60,607,815

Millions of Dollars

FIG. A.4.   PROJECTED NET INCOME, 1975–79
(Based on 1970–74 compound annual growth rate of 24.7%)

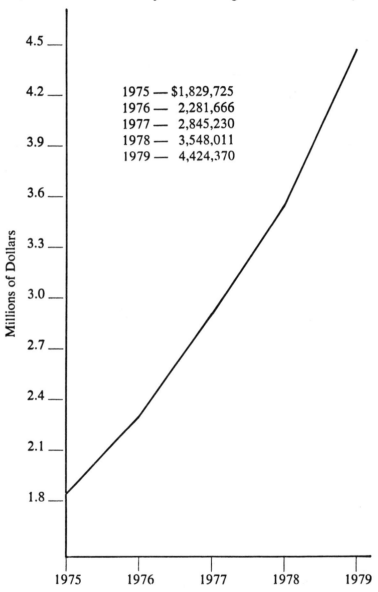

1975 — $1,829,725
1976 — 2,281,666
1977 — 2,845,230
1978 — 3,548,011
1979 — 4,424,370

FIG. A.5.   GRAPHIC LEVERAGE ANALYSIS, 1970–80

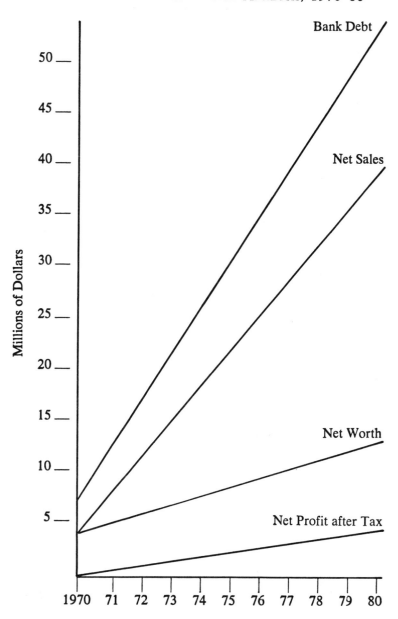

TABLE A.4. DATA RESOURCES FORECAST OF THE U.S. ECONOMY, 1975–80
(Billions of Dollars)

	1975	1976	1977	1978	1979	1980
Total Consumption	972.43	1,072.03	1,182.81	1,293.11	1,405.82	1,518.83
Durables (Total)	146.72	162.16	184.33	203.81	223.90	241.48
Nondurables	413.35	450.30	490.64	531.16	572.02	612.92
Services	412.36	459.56	507.85	558.13	609.90	664.43
Business Fixed Investment	166.87	181.85	207.20	234.43	257.88	279.84
Equipment	108.63	119.60	137.38	154.59	170.48	185.16
Nonresidential Construction	58.24	62.25	69.82	79.84	87.41	94.68
Inventory Investment	8.77	9.57	10.47	12.47	13.33	13.75
Net Exports	.50	.66	.42	.28	.76	1.54
Federal Military	84.32	89.37	95.68	103.14	111.63	120.70
Federal Civilian	41.70	44.35	47.88	52.45	57.96	64.08
State and Local	218.23	243.02	271.22	304.49	341.44	381.14
Gross National Product	1,548.38	1,707.94	1,890.62	2,079.83	2,273.45	2,467.37
Annual Growth (%)	10.4	10.3	10.7	10.0	9.3	8.5
Real GNP (1958 Dollars)	853.1	885.2	931.5	979.2	1,024.1	1,063.3
Annual Growth (%)	2.6	3.8	5.2	5.1	4.6	3.8

APPENDIX B
REPRESENTATIVE
LIST OF COMPANIES
THAT HAVE ADOPTED
ESOT PLANS

INDUSTRY	COMPANY
Advertising	The Katz Agency, Inc. Mr. Sam Jones, President 245 Park Avenue New York, New York 10017
Apparel Manufacturing	Jerell, Inc. Mr. Gerald Frankel, President 1365 Regal Row Dallas, Texas 75247
Architecture	Sasaki, Walker, Roberts and Associates, Inc. Mr. Peter Walker, President 2200 Bridgeway Boulevard Sausalito, California 94965
Box Manufacturing	J & J Corrugated Box Corp. Mr. Edwin A. Jaffee, President 201 Grove Street Franklin, Massachusetts 02038
Candy Manufacturing	Charms Company Walter W. Reid III, President Halls Mill Road Freehold, New Jersey 07728
Cement Manufacturing	Monolith Portland Cement Mr. Paul L. Schoonover, President 3326 San Fernando Road Glassell Station Los Angeles, California 90065

INDUSTRY	COMPANY
Civil Engineering	Gonzales & Oberkamper, Inc. Mr. Carlos E. Gonzales, President 10 Paul Drive San Rafael, California 94903
Commercial Photography and Advertising	Alderman Company Mr. Lewis C. Ferretti, V.P. Finance 2055 Francis Street High Point, North Carolina 27261
Construction	Egan & Sons Company Mr. C. E. Egan, President 7100 Medicine Lake Road Minneapolis, Minnesota 55427
Construction	University Industries Richard B. Huntington, President 4464 Alvarado Freeway San Diego, California 92120
Electrical Products Manufacturing	Gulf Consolidated Services, Inc. Mr. Keith Dorman, Ex. Vice President 2326 Transco Tower 2700 South Post Oak Road Houston, Texas 77027
Electronics Manufacturing	E-Systems, Inc. Mr. John Dixon, President P.O. Box 6030 Dallas, Texas 75222
Electronics Manufacturing	Intelcom Industries, Inc. Mr. Robert A. Berry, President P.O. Box 80817 San Diego, California 92138
Electronics Manufacturing	Ultra-Violet Products Mr. Thomas S. Warren, Chairman 5114 Walnut Grove Avenue San Gabriel, California 91778

INDUSTRY	COMPANY
Equipment Manufacturing	Steiger Tractor, Inc. Mr. Jack E. Johnson, President 5 North 23rd Street Fargo, North Dakota 58102
Food—Processing and Distribution of	Juice Bowl Products, Inc. Mr. John P. Grady, President P.O. Box 1048 Lakeland, Florida 33802
Freight Forwarding	Behring International, Inc. Mr. Alan I. Newhouse, President 1314 Texas Avenue Houston, Texas 77002
Greeting Card Manufacturing	Hallmark Cards, Inc. Mr. Donald J. Hall, President 25th and McGee Traffic Way Kansas City, Missouri 64108
Insurance	The Statesman Group, Inc. Mr. H. E. Clendenen, President Des Moines Building Des Moines, Iowa 50309
Insurance Brokerage	Kindler, Laucci & Day (CIMIC) Mr. Arthur H. Kindler, President 320 California Street San Francisco, California 94104
Lumber Manufacturing	Sacramento Valley Moulding Co. Mr. William Burford, President P.O. Box 62 Crescent Mills, California 95934
Lumber Retailing	MacBeath Hardwood Company Mr. William MacBeath, President 2150 Oakdale Avenue San Francisco, California 90017

INDUSTRY	COMPANY
Management Consulting	Manalytics, Inc. Mr. Elliot Schrier, President 425 Third Street San Francisco, California 94118
Mobile Home Sales	Woodland Mobile Homes, Inc. Mr. Larry Borgia, President 2350 El Camino Real Mountain View, California 94040
Oil Products Manufacturing	Phillips Products Company Division of Phillips Petroleum Co. Mr. Douglas Sherwin, Gen. Manager Suite 466, City Center Building Ann Arbor, Michigan 48104
Photographic Equipment Manufacturing	Helix Corporation Mr. Paul L. Schutt, President 679 N. Orleans Chicago, Illinois 60610
Printing	The Clegg Company Mr. William C. Clegg, Jr., President 130 Soledad Avenue San Antonio, Texas 78205
Printing	ESOT Printers, Inc. Mr. Donald Bumgarner, President 352 West 12th Avenue Eugene, Oregon 97401
Publishing	Peninsula Newspapers, Inc. Mr. Gene Bishop, President 630 Cowper Avenue Palo Alto, California 94301
Sawmill Equipment Manufacturing	Albany International Industries, Inc. Mr. Rene Fritz, Jr. P.O. Box 788 Albany, Oregon 97321

INDUSTRY	COMPANY
Steel Manufacturing	Mulach Steel Corporation Mr. J. F. Mulach, President 100 Hickory Grade Road Bridgeville, Pennsylvania 15107
Stock Brokerage	Merrill Lynch & Co., Inc. D. T. Regan, Chairman 165 Broadway New York, New York 10017
Stock Brokerage	Robinson-Humphrey Co., Inc. Mr. Justus C. Martin, Jr., President Two Peachtree Street N.W. Atlanta, Georgia 30303
Stock Brokerage	Sutro & Co., Inc. Mr. Ross Cobb, President 460 Montgomery Street San Francisco, California 94104
Textile Manufacturing	Halmode Apparel, Inc. Mr. Herbert S. Kurshan, President 230 Center Avenue N.W. Roanoke, Virginia 24007
Textile Manufacturing	Rockland Industries Mr. Zandy Leaderman, President Brooklandville, Maryland 21022

APPENDIX C
FORMS FOR
FAMILY ESTATE PLANNING

TABLE C.1.   PERSONAL DATA

Husband: _____
    (name)   (birthdate)   (insurable?)   (if not, why?)

Wife: _____
    (name)   (birthdate)   (insurable?)   (if not, why?)

RESIDENCE

Home address: _____ Since: _____

Business address: _____ Since: _____

Second home: _____ Since: _____

How long have you resided in state? _____

Prior residences: _____

_____

_____

_____

CITIZENSHIP, NATIONALITY, AND RELIGIOUS PREFERENCE

Husband: _____

Wife: _____

224

Table C.1—*Continued*

DEPENDENTS

Name	Address	Born	Marital Status

MARITAL HISTORY

Date of marriage _____ in state of _____

Terms of settlement if prior marriage and/or divorce accrued to either spouse: attach documentation if available.

TABLE C.2. PRESENT AND FUTURE CASH DEMANDS

INCOME SOURCES (NET FACTORS)

	Husband	Wife
Business profits (sole proprietorship)	_____	_____
Dividends and capital gains	_____	_____
Interest—taxable and nontaxable	_____	_____
Net, rents	_____	_____
Miscellaneous sources	_____	_____
Royalties—gas, oil, and other	_____	_____
Salaries	_____	_____
Trusts (attach exhibits/agreements)	_____	_____
Total		

CURRENT EXPENSES

	Husband	Wife
Insurance premiums—life and general	_____	_____
Mortgage and contract payments	_____	_____
Living expenses	_____	_____
Other expenditures	_____	_____
Tax liabilities—real property	_____	_____
Tax liabilities—federal and state	_____	_____
Total		

REMAINDER AVAILABLE FOR CONSERVATION

(Revenue sources less current expenses)

Total

Table C.2.—*Continued*

FUTURE REVENUE SOURCES
(after retirement)

		Husband	Wife
Annuities and insurance		_____	_____
Dividends and capital gains		_____	_____
Employer retirement benefits		_____	_____
Interest—taxable and nontaxable		_____	_____
Miscellaneous sources		_____	_____
Other employee benefits		_____	_____
Other investment return (identify)		_____	_____
Social Security benefits		_____	_____
Trusts		_____	_____
	Total		

FUTURE CASH REQUIREMENTS
(after retirement)

		Husband	Wife
Living expenses		_____	_____
Mortgage and contract payments		_____	_____
Other expenditures		_____	_____
Tax liabilities—federal and state		_____	_____
Tax liabilities—real property		_____	_____
	Total		

REMAINDER AVAILABLE FOR
CONSERVATION AND RETENTION
(Future revenue sources less
   future cash requirements)

Total	

TABLE C.3.   SUMMARY OF FAMILY
ASSETS AND LIABILITIES

	Husband	Wife	Joint
			(identify contributor H/W)
PRESENT ASSETS			
Bonds (Exhibit I)	_____	_____	_____

Table C.3.—*Continued*

	Husband	Wife	Joint
Cash in banks (Exhibit I)			
Closely held business interests (Exhibit II)			
Employee benefits (Exhibit V)			
Insurance (Exhibit IV)			
Stocks and mutual funds (Exhibit I)			
Miscellaneous assets (Exhibit VI)			
Notes, accounts receivable, mortgages (Exhibit I)			
Real estate (Exhibit III)			
Total			

CURRENT FIXED LIABILITIES

(Exhibit VII)

	Husband	Wife	Joint
Charitable pledges			
Insurance policy loans			
Notes to financial institutions			
Other obligations			
Real estate mortgages			
Tax liabilities, federal and state			
Total			

FAMILY NET WORTH
(Assets minus liabilities)

Total

TABLE C.4. INFORMATION SOURCES
FAMILY CONSULTANTS

	Name	Address	Telephone
Accountant:			
Banker:			
Doctor:			
Executor:			
Lawyer:			
Life insurance agent:			
Financial consultant:			
Stockbroker:			
Trust officer:			

CURRENT FAMILY TAX-PLANNING INFORMATION/DOCUMENTS

Income tax returns—where filed? _____
(attach last year's copy)
Gift tax returns—where filed? _____

Lifetime marital deduction? _____
(attach copy)

Other pertinent information:
  Husband's Social Security number _____
  Wife's Social Security number _____
  Safe deposit box number _____ Located _____
  Safe deposit box number _____ Located _____

Trusts:
  Trustee: _____ Revocable? Irrevocable? _____
  (attach exhibit and documents)

  Trustee: _____ Revocable? Irrevocable? _____
  (attach exhibit and documents)

Wills:
  Husband: _____
          (date)   (location)

  Wife: _____
          (date)   (location)

TABLE C.5. EXHIBIT I:
BONDS, BANKS, NOTES, ETC.

BONDS

Description	Ownership (H) or (W)	Original Cost	Present Value	Present Yield
_____	_____	_____	_____	_____
_____	_____	_____	_____	_____
_____	_____	_____	_____	_____
_____	_____	_____	_____	_____

CASH IN BANKS

	Name of Institution	Amount Husband	Wife	Joint
Checking account	_____	___	___	___
Checking account	_____	___	___	___
Checking account	_____	___	___	___
Checking account	_____	___	___	___
Savings account	_____	___	___	___
Savings account	_____	___	___	___
Savings account	_____	___	___	___
Savings account	_____	___	___	___

STOCKS

Description	Ownership (H) or (W)	Original Cost	Present Value	Present Yield
_____	_____	_____	_____	_____
_____	_____	_____	_____	_____
_____	_____	_____	_____	_____
_____	_____	_____	_____	_____

MUNICIPAL FUND SHARES

Description	Ownership	Original Cost	Present Value	Present Yield
_____	_____	_____	_____	_____
_____	_____	_____	_____	_____
_____	_____	_____	_____	_____

NOTES, ACCOUNTS RECEIVABLE, AND MORTGAGES

Debtor	Security/ Unsecured	Date of Maturity	Original Amount	Present Value
_____	_____	_____	_____	_____
_____	_____	_____	_____	_____
_____	_____	_____	_____	_____
_____	_____	_____	_____	_____

TABLE C.6. EXHIBIT II:
CLOSELY HELD BUSINESS INTERESTS

GENERAL DATA

1. Name of business: _____
2. Business address: _____
3. Type of business organization
   (regular corporation,
   subchapter S
   corporation, partnership,
   sole proprietorship): _____
4. Management consultant: _____

	(name)	(address)	(phone)

Accountant: _____

	(name)	(address)	(phone)

CAPITALIZATION (IF CORPORATION)

	Common	Preferred	Debt
Outstanding			
Authorized			
Return on investment			
Dividend history (rates)			

DISTRIBUTION OF OWNERSHIP

Husband			
Wife			
Children			
Others			

BUY/SELL AGREEMENT

1. Is there a buy/sell agreement? _____
2. If so, describe (cross-purchase,
   stock redemption, combination
   —attach copies): _____
3. How is the buy/sell funded? _____
4. Method for valuation purposes
   (book value, earnings multiple,
   appraisal, agreed value—
   attach copies): _____

OTHER COMMITMENTS OF BUSINESS

	Yes	No	Copies Attached
1. Deferred compensation agreement?			
2. Key-man insurance?			
3. Other employee benefit plans?			
4. Stock option agreement?			

TABLE C.7. EXHIBIT III:
REAL ESTATE—IRS 1250 PROPERTIES

	Parcel 1	Parcel 2	Parcel 3
GENERAL INFORMATION			
Location of property			
Type of property (residence, commercial, etc.)			
If joint property, show contribution by each joint tenant—how? when?			
Date property was acquired			
Cost basis of the property			
Present fair market value			
Date determined			
MORTGAGE CONTRACT AND INDEBTEDNESS			
Original mortgage			
Current amount of mortgage			
Amortization scheduling			
FAMILY FARMS			
Value of farm machinery and equipment			
Excess of land value over value of operating farm as a business—Tax Reform Act of 1976, 2003; Code 2032A			
CASH FLOW PRO FORMA SCHEDULE			
+Yearly gross income			
−Yearly maintenance costs			
−Yearly property taxes			
Yearly depreciation—method?			
−Debt payments (principal and interest)			
Results in + or − cash flow			

TABLE C.8. EXHIBIT IV:
LIFE INSURANCE

LIFE INSURANCE OWNED ON HUSBAND/WIFE

	Face Value	Policy Type	Premium	Cash Value	Beneficiary
Company: ____ No: ____					
Company: ____ No: ____					
Company: ____ No: ____					
Company: ____ No: ____					
Company: ____ No: ____					
Company: ____ No: ____					
Company: ____ No: ____					

LIFE INSURANCE OWNED ON OTHERS

Company: ____ No: ____					
Company: ____ No: ____					
Company: ____ No: ____					
Company: ____ No: ____					
Company: ____ No: ____					
Company: ____ No: ____					
Company: ____ No: ____					

TABLE C.9. EXHIBIT V:
RETIREMENT COMPENSATION
PROGRAMS AND EMPLOYEE BENEFITS

TYPE OF PLAN	Annual Dollar Retirement Benefit	Amount Contributed	Dollar Amount of Death Benefits
Deferred compensation	_____	_____	_____
Employee stock ownership plan	_____	_____	_____
H. G. 10 (Keogh plan)	_____	_____	_____
Individual retirement account	_____	_____	_____
Pension	_____	_____	_____
Profit sharing	_____	_____	_____

STOCK OPTION PLANS

	Option Price	Present Value
Qualified plan	_____	_____
Nonqualified plan	_____	_____

INSURANCE
Group life insurance

Amount of Benefit

Company _____ _____
Beneficiary _____
Company _____ _____
Beneficiary _____

Accident insurance
Company _____ _____
Beneficiary _____
Company _____ _____
Beneficiary _____

Health and medical insurance
Company _____ _____
Beneficiary _____
Company _____ _____
Beneficiary _____

TABLE C.10. EXHIBIT VI:
MISCELLANEOUS ASSETS

PERSONAL EFFECTS

	Husband	Wife	Jointly Owned
Clothing			
Furs			
Home furnishings			
Jewelry			

OTHER PERSONAL PROPERTY

Automobiles			
Other (boats, aircraft R.V.'s, office contents)			

ESTATES AND TRUSTS

Anticipated benefits			
Powers of appointment			

MINERAL INTERESTS

Oil and gas			
Other			

SOCIAL CLUB MEMBERSHIPS

TABLE C.11. EXHIBIT VII: FAMILY PERSONAL LIABILITIES

CHARITABLE PLEDGES

	Present Amount	Interest Rate
To: _____	_____	_____
To: _____	_____	_____
To: _____	_____	_____
To: _____	_____	_____
To: _____	_____	_____

INSURANCE POLICY LOANS

From: _____	_____	_____
From: _____	_____	_____
From: _____	_____	_____
From: _____	_____	_____
From: _____	_____	_____

NOTES TO FINANCIAL INSTITUTIONS

To: _____	_____	_____
To: _____	_____	_____
To: _____	_____	_____
To: _____	_____	_____
To: _____	_____	_____

OTHER OBLIGATIONS

To: _____	_____	_____
To: _____	_____	_____
To: _____	_____	_____
To: _____	_____	_____
To: _____	_____	_____

REAL ESTATE MORTGAGES

From: _____	_____	_____
From: _____	_____	_____
From: _____	_____	_____
From: _____	_____	_____
From: _____	_____	_____

TAX LIABILITIES

Federal: _____
State: _____

BIBLIOGRAPHY

Argyris, Chris. *Intervention Theory and Method: A Behavioral Science View*. Reading, Mass.: Addison-Wesley, 1970.

Bills, Charles W. *Valuation of Assets*. Washington, D.C.: Bureau of National Affairs, Inc., 1976.

Bushman, Ronald M. "Employee Stock Ownership Plans." *The Financial Planner*, December, 1974.

Ellentuck, Albert B. *Practical Merger Techniques for Buying and Selling a Business*. New York: Commerce Clearing House, 1974.

Elting, Charles E. *What Is Your Corporation Worth?* New York: Research Institute of America, Inc., 1974.

Frisch, Robert A. *The Magic of ESOT*. New York: Farnsworth Publishing Co., 1975.

Goodson, Marvin, ed. *The New Pension Legislation: ESOTs under ERISA—History and Analysis*. New York: Law Journal, 1975.

Jurek, Walter. *Successfully Buy, Sell, or Finance a Business*. Stow, Ohio: Walter Jurek and Associates Management Engineers, 1976.

Kelso, Louis O., and Hetter, Patricia, eds. *Two-Factor Theory: The Economics of Reality*. New York: Random House, 1967.

Kess, Sidney, and Westlin, Beril, eds. *Estate Planning Guide*. Chicago: Commerce Clearing House, 1976.

McLean, John G. "How to Evaluate New Capital Investments." In *Harvard Business Review on Management*, edited by C. L. Dingler. New York: Harper & Row, 1975.

Packwood, Robert. "Minimum Tax, Limitations on Artificial Accounting Losses and Related Provisions." Review and Research Letter, July 1, 1976.

Phillipp, James G., ed. *Fiduciary Responsibility*. New York: Law Journal, 1975.

Pillsbury, Charles A., ed. *Employee Stock Ownership Plans: A Step toward Democratic Capitalism*. New York: Law Journal, 1975.

Rabkin, Jacob, and Johnson, Mark H., eds. *Federal Income, Gift and Estate Taxation*. 7 Vols. New York: Matthew Bender, 1976.

Sherman, Howard J., and Hunt, E. K., eds. *Economics—An Introduction to Traditional and Radical Views*. New York: Harper & Row, 1972.

Stafford, Walter V., ed. *Securities and Corporate Planning Considerations*. New York: Law Journal, 1975.

Thomas, Dana L. "Explosive ESOTS." *Barron's National Business and Financial Weekly*, July 28, 1975.

U.S. Congress. House of Representatives. Committee on Finance, Subcommittee on ESOP Purpose. No. 98-1280. 93d Cong., 2nd Sess. 313, 1974. Washington, D.C.: U.S. Government Printing Office, 1974.

U.S. Congress. Senate. Committee on Finance. *Regional Rail Reorganization Act of 1975*. Hearing, 94th Cong., 1st Sess., February 26, 1975. Washington, D.C.: U.S. Government Printing Office, 1975.

U.S. Congress. Senate. Committee on Finance. *The Reorganization of Northeast Railroads. Hearing*. 119th Cong., December 11, 1973. Washington, D.C.: U.S. Government Printing Office, 1973.

U.S. Department of the Treasury. Internal Revenue Service. *Internal Revenue Code of 1954*, subchapter D., "Deferred Compensation" (1976) Sections 401-25.

U.S. Department of the Treasury. Internal Revenue Service. *Internal Revenue Ruling 71-311*, 1971-2 CB.

West, James E., and Prather, Charles L., eds. *Financing Business Firms*. Homewood, Ill.: Richard D. Irwin, 1975.

INDEX

239